Fun & Games

SHORT FICTIONS

BOOKS BY CLARENCE MAJOR

FUN & GAMES

PAINTED TURTLE: WOMAN WITH GUITAR

SUCH WAS THE SEASON

MY AMPUTATIONS

EMERGENCY EXIT

REFLEX AND BONE STRUCTURE

NO

ALL-NIGHT VISITORS

SURFACES AND MASKS

SOME OBSERVATIONS OF A STRANGER AT ZUNI IN THE
  LATTER PART OF THE CENTURY

INSIDE DIAMETER: THE FRANCE POEMS

THE SYNCOPATED CAKEWALK

THE COTTON CLUB

PRIVATE LINE

SYMPTOMS & MADNESS

SWALLOW THE LAKE

DICTIONARY OF AFRO-AMERICAN SLANG

THE DARK AND FEELING

Fun & Games

SHORT FICTIONS

by

Clarence Major

HOLY COW! PRESS
DULUTH, MINNESOTA 1990

LIBRARY OF CONGRESS CATALOGING-IN-PUBLICATION DATA

Major, Clarence
  Fun & Games : short fictions / by Clarence Major, —1st ed.
    p.   cm.
  I. Title. II. Title: Fun and games.
PS3563.A39F86   1990   88-45370
813'.54—dc20   CIP
ISBN 0-930100-34-4

FIRST EDITION
10 9 8 7 6 5 4 3 2 1

Some of the stories included herein have previously appeared in the following publications. We gratefully acknowledge reprint permission. "Party with Masks" (*The Agni Review*), "Marilyn" (*The Black Scholar*), "My Mother and Mitch" (*Boulevard*), "Maggy: A Woman of the King" (*Departures: Contemporary Arts Review*), "Ten Pecan Pies" (*Essence*), "The Vase and the Rose" (*par rapport: a journal of the humanities*), "Fun and Games" (*Seattle Review*), and "Mobile Axis: A Triptych" (*Witness*).

Publisher's Address: Distributor's Address:
Holy Cow! Press   The Talman Company, Inc.
Post Office Box 3170   150 Fifth Avenue
Mount Royal Station   New York, New York
Duluth, Minnesota 55803   10011

This project is supported, in part, by a grant from the National Endowment for the Arts in Washington, D.C., a Federal agency.

Contents

I

My Mother and Mitch

H E WAS JUST SOMEBODY who had dialed the wrong number. This is how it started and I wasn't concerned about it. Not at first. I don't even remember if I was there when he first called but I do, all these many years later, remember my mother on the phone speaking to him in her best quiet voice, trying to sound as ladylike as she knew how.

She had these different voices for talking to different people on different occasions. I could tell by my mother's proper voice that this man was somebody she wanted to make a good impression on, a man she thought she might like to know. This was back when my mother was still a young woman, divorced but still young enough to believe that she was not completely finished with men. She was a skeptic from the beginning, I knew that even then. But some part of her thought the right man might come along some day.

I don't know exactly what it was about him that attracted her though. People are too mysterious to know that well. I know that now and I must have been smart enough not to wonder too hard about it back then.

Since I remember hearing her tell him her name she must not have given it out right off the bat when he first called. She was a city woman with a child and had developed a certain alertness to danger. One thing you didn't do was give your name to a stranger on the phone. You never knew who to trust in a city like Chicago. The place was full of crazy people and criminals.

She said, "My name is *Mrs.* Jayne Anderson." I can still hear her laying the emphasis on the Mrs. although she had been separated from my father twelve years by 1951 when this man dialed her number by accident.

Mitch Kibbs was the name he gave her. I guess he must have told her who he was the very first time, just after he apologized for calling her by mistake. I can't remember who he was trying to call. He must have told her and she must have told me but it's gone now. I think they must have talked a pretty good while that first time. The first thing that I remember about him was that he lived with his sister who was older than he. The next thing was that he was very old. He must have been fifty and to me at fifteen that was deep into age. If my mother was old at thirty, fifty was ancient. Then the other thing about him was that he was white.

They'd talked five or six times I think before he came out and said he was white but she knew it before he told her. I think he made this claim only after he started suspecting he might not be talking to another white person. But the thing was he didn't know for sure she was black. I was at home lying on the couch pretending to read a magazine when I heard her say, "I am a colored lady." Those were her words exactly. She placed her emphasis on the word lady.

I had never known my mother to date any white men. She would hang up from talking with him and she and I would sit at the kitchen table and she'd tell me what he'd said. They were telling each other the bits and pieces of their lives, listening to each other, feeling their way as they talked. She spoke slowly, remembering all the details. I watched her scowl and the way her eyes narrowed as she puzzled over his confessions as she told me in her own words about them. She was especially puzzled about his reaction to her confession about being colored.

That night she looked across at me with that fearful look that was hers alone and said, "Tommy, I doubt if he will ever call back. Not after tonight. He didn't know. You know that."

Feeling grown-up because she was treating me that way, I said, "I wouldn't be so sure."

But he called back soon after that.

I was curious about her interest in this particular old white man so I always listened carefully. I was a little bit scared too because I suspected he might be some kind of maniac or pervert. I had no good reason to fear such a thing except that I thought it strange that anybody could spend as much time as he and my mother did talking on the phone without any desire for human contact. She had never had a telephone relationship before and at that time all I knew about telephone relationships was that they were insane and conducted by people who probably needed to be put away. This meant that I also had the sad feeling that my mother was a bit crazy too. But more important than these fearful fantasies, I thought I was witnessing a change in my mother. It seemed important and I didn't want to misunderstand it or miss the point of it. I tried to look on the bright side which was what my mother always said I should try to do.

He certainly didn't sound dangerous. Two or three times I myself answered the phone when he called and he always said, "Hello, Tommy, this is Mitch, may I speak to your mother," and I always said, "Sure, just a minute." He never asked me how I was doing or anything like that and I never had anything special to say to him.

After he'd been calling for over a month I sort of lost interest in hearing about their talk. But she went right on telling me what he said. I was a polite boy so I listened despite the fact that I had decided that Mitch Kibbs and his ancient sister Temple Erikson were crazy but harmless. My poor mother was lonely. That was all. I had it all figured out. He wasn't an ax murderer who was going to sneak up on her one evening when she was coming home from her job at the factory and split her open from the top down. We were always hearing about things like this so I knew it wasn't impossible.

My interest would pick up occasionally. I was especially interested in what happened the first time my mother herself made the call to his house. She told me that Temple Erikson answered the phone. Mother and I were eating dinner when she started talking about Temple Erikson.

"She's a little off in the head."

I didn't say anything but it confirmed my suspicion. What surprised me was my mother's ability to recognize it. "What'd she say?"

"She rattled on about the Wild West and the Indians and having to hide in a barrel or something like that. Said the Indians were shooting arrows at them and she was just a little girl who hid in a barrel."

I thought about this. "Maybe she lived out west when she was young. You know? She must be a hundred by now. That would make her the right age."

"Oh, come on, now. What she said was she married when she was fourteen, married this Erikson fellow. As near as I could figure out he must have been a leather tanner but seems he also hunted fur and sold it to make a living. She never had a child."

"None of that sounds crazy." I was disappointed.

"She was talking crazy, though."

"How so?"

"She thinks the Indians are coming back to attack the house any day now. She says things like Erikson was still living, like he was just off there in the next room, taking a nap. One of the first things Mitch told me was his sister and he moved in together after her husband died and that was twenty years ago."

"How did the husband die?"

"Huh?"

"How did he die?"

She finished chewing her peas first. "Kicked in the head by a horse. Bled to death."

I burst out laughing because the image was so bright in my mind and I couldn't help myself. My pretty mother had a sense of humor even when she didn't mean to show it.

She chewed her peas in a ladylike manner. This was long before she lost her teeth. Sitting there across the table from her I knew I loved her and needed her and I knew she loved and needed me. I was not yet fearing that she needed me too much. She had a lot of anger in her too. Men had hurt her bad. And one day I was going to be a man.

When I laughed my mother said, "You shouldn't laugh at misfortune, Tommy." But she had this silly grin on her face and it caused me to crack up again. I just couldn't stop. I think now I must have been a bit hysterical from the anxiety I had been living with all those weeks while she was telling me about the telephone conversations that I wanted to hear about only part of the time.

It was dark outside and I got up when I finished my dinner and went to the window and looked down on the streetlights glowing in the wet pavement. I said, "I bet he's out there right now, hiding in the shadows, watching our window."

"Who?" Her eyes grew large. She was easily frightened. I knew this and I was being devilish and deliberately trying to scare her.

"You know, Mister Kibbs."

She looked relieved. "No he's not. He's not like that. He's a little strange but not a pervert."

"How'd you know?"

By the look she gave me I knew now that I had thrown doubt into her and she wasn't handling it well. She didn't try to answer me. She finished her small, dry pork chop and the last of her bright green peas and reached over and took up my plate and sat it inside of her own.

She took the dishes to the sink, turned on the hot and cold water so that warm water gushed out of the single faucet, causing the pipe to clang, and started washing the dishes. "You have a vivid imagination," was all she said.

I grabbed the dishcloth and started drying the first plate she placed in the rack. "Even so, you don't know this man. You never even seen him. Aren't you curious about what he looks like?"

"I know what he looks like."

"How?"

"He sent me a picture of himself and one of Temple."

I gave her a look. She had been holding out on me. I knew he was crazy now. Was he so ugly she hadn't wanted me to see the picture? I ask if I could see it.

She dried her hands on the cloth I was holding then took her cigarettes out of her dress pocket and knocked one from the pack and stuck it between her thin pale lips. I watched her light it and fan the smoke and squint her eyes. She said, "You have to promise not to laugh."

That did it. I started laughing again and couldn't stop. Then she started laughing too because I was bent double, standing there at the sink, with this image of some old guy who looked like The Creeper in my mind. But I knew she couldn't read my mind so she had to be laughing at me laughing. She was still young enough to be silly with me like a kid.

Then she brought out two pictures, one of him and the other one of his sister. She put them down side by side on the table. "Make sure your hands are dry."

I took off my glasses and bent down to the one of the man first so I could see up close as I stood there wiping my hands on the dishcloth. It was one of those studio pictures where somebody had posed him in a three-quarter view. He had his unruly hair and eyebrows pasted down and you could tell he was fresh out of the bath and his white shirt was starched hard. He was holding his scrubbed face with effort toward where the photographer told him to look which was too much in the direction of the best light. He was frowning with discomfort beneath the forced smile. There was something else. It was something like defeat or simple tiredness in his pose and you could see it best in the heavy lids of his large blank eyes. He looked out of that face at the world with what remained of his self-confidence and trust in the world. His shaggy presence said that it was all worth while and maybe even in some ways he would not ever understand also important. I understood all of that even then but would never have been able to put my reading of him into words like these.

Then I looked at the woman. She was an old hawk. Her skin was badly wrinkled like the skin of ancient Indians I'd seen in photographs and the westerns. There was something like a smile coming out of her face but it had come out sort of sideways and made her look silly. But the main thing about her was that she looked very mean. But on second thought, to give her the benefit of the doubt, I can say that it might have been just plain hardness from having had a hard life. She was wearing a black iron-stiff dress buttoned up to her dickey which was ironically dainty and tight around her goose neck.

All I said was, "They're *so* old." I don't know what else I thought as I looked up at my mother who was leaning over my shoulder looking at the pictures too, as though she'd never seen them before, as though she was trying to see them through my eyes.

"You're just young, Tommy. Everybody's old to you. They're not so old. He looks lonely, to me."

I looked at him again and thought I saw what she meant.

I put the dishes away and she took the photographs back and we didn't talk any more that night about Mitch and Temple. We watched our black-and-white television screen which showed us Red Skelton acting like a fool.

Before it was over, I fell asleep on the couch and my mother woke me when she turned off the television. "You should go to bed."

I stood up and stretched. "I have a science paper to write."

"Get up early and write it," she said, putting out her cigarette.

"He wants me to meet him someplace," my mother said.

She had just finished talking with him and was standing by the telephone. It was close to dinner time. I'd been home from school since three-thirty and she'd been in from work by then for a good hour. She'd just hung up from the shortest conversation she'd ever had with him.

I'd wondered why they never wanted to meet then I stopped wondering and felt glad they hadn't. Now I was afraid, afraid for her, for myself, for the poor old man in the picture. Why did we have to go through with this crazy thing?

"I told him I needed to talk with you about it first," she said. "I told him I'd call him back."

I was standing there in front of her looking at her. She was a scared little girl with wild eyes dancing in her head, unable to make up her own mind. I sensed her fear. I resented her for the mess she had gotten herself in. I also resented her for needing my consent. I knew she wanted me to say go, go to him, meet him somewhere. I could tell. She was too curious not to want to go. I suddenly thought that he might be a millionaire and that she would marry the old coot and he'd die and leave her his fortune. But there was the sister. She was in the way. And from the looks of her she would pass herself off as one of the living for at least another hundred years or so. So I gave up that fantasy.

"Well, why don't you tell him you'll meet him at the hamburger cafe on Wentworth? We can eat dinner there."

"We?"

"Sure. I'll just sit at the counter like I don't know you. But I gotta be there to protect you."

"I see."

"Then you can walk in alone. I'll already be there eating a cheeseburger and fries. He'll come in and see you waiting for him alone at a table."

"No, I'll sit at the counter too," she said.

"Okay. You sit at the counter too."

"What time should I tell him?"

I looked at my Timex. It was six. I knew they lived on the West Side and that meant it would take him at least an hour by bus and a half hour by car. He probably didn't have a car. I was hungry though and had already set my mind on eating a cheeseburger rather than macaroni and cheese out of the box.

"Tell him seven-thirty."

"Okay."

I went to my room. I didn't want to hear her talking to him in her soft whispering voice. I'd stopped listening some time before. I looked at the notes for homework and felt sick in the stomach at the thought of having to write that science paper.

A few minutes later my mother came in and said, "Okay. It's all set." She sat down on the side of my bed and folded her bony pale hands in her lap. "What should I wear?"

"Wear your green dress and the brown shoes."

"You like that dress don't you."

"I like that one and the black one with the yellow at the top. It's classical."

"You mean classy."

"Whatever I mean." I felt really grown that night.

"Here, Tommy, take this." She handed me five dollars which she'd been hiding in the palm of her right hand. "Don't spend it all. Buy the burger out of it and the rest is just to have. If you spend it all in that hamburger place I'm going to deduct it from your allowance next week."

When I got there I changed my mind about the counter. I took a table by myself.

I was eating my cheeseburger and watching the revolving door. The cafe was noisy with shouts, cackling, giggles and verbal warfare. The waitress, Miss Azibo, was in a bad mood. She'd set my hamburger plate down like it was burning her hand.

I kept my eye on the door. Every time somebody came in I looked up, every time somebody left I looked up. I finished my cheeseburger even before my mother got there, and, ignoring her warning, I ordered another and another Coca-Cola to go with it. I figured I could eat two or three burgers and still have most of the five left.

Then my mother came in like a bright light into a dingy room. I think she must have been the most beautiful woman who ever entered that place and it was her first time coming in there. She had always been something of a snob and did not believe in places like this. I knew she'd agreed to meet Mister Kibbs here just because she believed in my right to the cheeseburger and this place had the best in the neighborhood.

I watched her walk ladylike to the counter and ease herself up on the stool and sit there with her back arched. People in that place didn't walk and sit like that. She was acting classy and everybody turned to look at her. I looked around at the faces and a lot of the women had these real mean sneering looks like somebody had broke wind.

She didn't know any of these people and they didn't know her. Some of them may have known her by sight, and me too, but that was about all the contact we had with this part of the neighborhood. Besides, we hardly ever ate out. When we did we usually ate Chinese or at the rib place.

I sipped my Coke and watched Miss Azibo place a cup of coffee before my mother on the counter. She was a coffee freak. Always was. All day long. Long into the night. Cigarettes and coffee in a continuous cycle. I grew up with her that way. The harsh smells are still in my memory. When she picked up the cup with a dainty finger sticking out just so, I heard a big fat woman at a table in front of mine say to the big fat woman at the table with her that my mother was a snooty bitch. The other woman said, "Yeah. She must thank she's white. What she doing in here anyway?"

Mitch Kibbs came in about twenty minutes after my mother and I watched him stop and stand just inside the revolving doors. He stood to the side. He looked a lot younger than in the picture. He was stooped a bit though and he wasn't dressed like a million-aire which disappointed me. But he was clean. He was wearing a necktie and a clean white shirt and a suit that looked like it was about two hundred years old but one no doubt made of the best wool. Although it was fall he looked over-dressed for the season. He looked like a man who hadn't been out in daylight in a long while. He was nervous, I could tell. Everybody was looking at him. Rarely did white people come in here.

Then he went to my mother like he knew she had to be the person he'd come in to see. He sat himself up on the stool beside her and leaned forward with his elbows on the counter and looked in her face.

She looked back in that timid way of hers. But she wasn't timid. It was an act and part of her ladylike posture. She used it when she needed it.

They talked and talked. I sat there eating cheeseburgers and protecting her till I spent the whole five dollars. Even as I ran out of money I knew she would forgive me. She had always forgiven me on special occasions. This was one for sure.

She never told me what they talked about in the cafe and I never asked but everything that happened after that meeting went to-ward the finishing off of the affair my mother was having with Mitch Kibbs. He called her later that night. I was in my room reading when the phone rang and I could hear her speaking to him in that ladylike way — not the way she talked to me. I was differ-ent. She didn't need to impress me. I was her son. But I couldn't hear what she was saying and didn't want to.

Mister Kibbs called the next evening too. But eventually the calls were fewer and fewer till he no longer called.

My mother and I went on living the way we always had, she working long hours at the factory and me going to school. She was not a happy woman but I thought she was pretty brave. Every once in a while she got invited somewhere, to some wedding or out on a date with a man. She always tried on two or three different dresses, turning herself around and around before the mirror, asking me how she looked, making me select the dress she would wear. Most often though she went nowhere. After dinner we sat together at the kitchen table, she drinking coffee and smoking her eternal cigarettes. She gave me my first can of beer one night when she herself felt like having one. It tasted awful and I didn't touch the stuff for years after that.

About a day or two after the meeting in the hamburger cafe I remember coming to a conclusion about my mother. I learned for the first time that she did not always know what she was doing. It struck me that she was as helpless as I sometimes felt when confronted with a math or science problem or a problem about sex and girls and growing up and life in general. She didn't know everything. And that made me feel closer to her despite the fear it caused. She was there to protect me, I thought. But there she was, just finding her way, step by step, like me. It was something wonderful anyway.

Saving the Children

1

Y OU CAN TRY AND you can try to do what's right for folks and
sometimes it just seems like nothing you do turns out right.
And you gets misunderstood, too. It ain't easy, this life. No, sir.

At the time, we lived in the church itself.

It was a pretty little church right at the corner of Coca-Cola
Place and Pratt Street. Had a fresh coat of white paint and somebody had done painted the shutters and the front doors cabbage-
green. I was proud of Zora.

We had cold days that summer and the winter fore that the days
was real hot. Zora said all them bombs they dropped over in Europe had done changed the seasons and God was angry with them
all for messing up the sky. But the war was over by then and had
been for two whole years.

With the Lord's help, we was doing pretty well for the first time
in my memory.

At the time Scoop came in with Juneboy and Lauren, me and
Zora was in the church polishing up the pulpit with Johnson's
Wax. I member it was a Wednesday cause that's the day I take in
wash and I had a big pile of it out back. It was bout three in the
afternoon. Reverend Hunter wont there less he was in his room
at the front and the fact skipped my mind.

14

"Well, well, well," said Zora when she turned and saw Scoop and the children coming up the aisle.

They came in so quiet-like but you know you can feel a presence approaching on you. My son Scoop always been a soft walker and a quiet talker. Gets it honest. More from me than his daddy. I never been much for talking cept in my own head to myself and I go bout my business doing that all the time, just a carrying on my own conversations, mostly with the Lord, planning my journey, walking up that last road.

"Lord, ain't yall a sight for sore eyes," said Zora.

She was looking down at the children.

I wiped my hands on my apron. "Pretty as can be."

Scoop was grinning like a fool with his gold tooth bright as a sunrise. "Ain't you gon give your grandmomma a big hug?"

He was talking to both of them.

Juneboy looked up at his daddy like he didn't know what that meant while Lauren held her arms toward me. I bent my old back and pulled the child to me and patted her on the head. She was big for her age, which was nine, and almost up to my shoulder.

Scoop pushed Juneboy over and I pulled him to me too.

Zora said, "You bring their clothes?"

"In the car."

"Ain't yall gone hug your Aunt Zora?" Zora got that whine in her voice like her feelings been hurt.

She squanched down and hugged the two babies. Juneboy looked like he was the baby he was so small. He kinda pulled back from Zora like he didn't like her but, my, how that boy looked like her, just like she done spit him out of her own mouth. Standing betwixt her and his own momma nobody woulda picked his momma for the one that birthed him.

"You all right, Scoop?"

"Oh, yeah. I'm fine, Momma. Don't worry bout me. I'll straighten everything out and take them back in a week or two. I got to find a place first. I'm working on it. Got my scouts out." He laughed and wagged his head.

"You ain't in no trouble is you?"

"No, Momma, no. The only trouble I got is getting and keeping dependable waitresses to work the counter." He shook his head. "No, no. I'm fine, personally fine. I'm just looking for a bigger place. It ain't proper for the three of us to sleep in the same bed — Lauren being a girl. That's all."

"Reverend Hunter might know somebody with a place."

"Oh, no, Zora. I wouldn't bother him. Besides, I got a lead already."

"Well," said Zora, "with the Lord's help, Momma and I will do all in our might to give these youngsters a proper upbringing, Scoop. God knows they been neglected far too long."

I seed him studying what she just said then it sunk in and he said, "Oh, I'm not leaving them for good. I'll be back to take them, Zora. I know you'd make a good home for my babies but I couldn't leave them on you *all* the time."

I said, "Won't be no bother, son, if Zora say so. This her church, hers and the Reverend's. Your sister is a pastor, too, you know. Ain't it pretty?"

Scoop turned and looked left to the pretty painted windows with scenes of Christ in the stages of his life then to the other side at the other scenes then shook his head yes, but looking kinda shame of hisself cause, you know, he just wont the church-going type and I know my boy — he was feeling shame of hisself for backsliding so many times he had give up trying to come back to the Lord.

We was standing right there in front of the pulpit by the banister that runs round it. Zora grinned at her little brother and said, "Now that we got our *own* church in the family you should start coming back to service, Scoop."

"Yeah, I guess I should."

"You should, son," I said.

"Yeah, I know I should."

The children squirmed away and Juneboy started running his finger long the wood and humming to himself. Lauren watched us talk. She was always more interested in grownups than Juneboy.

"Don't rub your dirty hands on that banister, Juneboy," Zora said in her scorning voice, "Grandmomma and I just polished it all pretty and besides, the Lord wouldn't want you to mess up his temple." She gets this way of talking sometimes in the pulpit when she trying to get the congregation to know she means business, shaking her Bible at them. "Go out in the backyard and play, if you got to play the minute you get here, even before you say howdy do."

I seed Juneboy get all hurt inside and I knowed Zora spoke too hard to the boy but she didn't mean no harm. She got a heart of gold. Nothing on earth she wont do for them children. But he was too little to understand. Peoples don't pay children much mind, I know, but I do. I always member my own self when I was little and how much I used to cry just trying to stay alive and keep the hurt from killing me. I didn't say nothing when Juneboy went to his daddy and leaned ginst his leg, the tears coming to his big old lost eyes. Scoop rubbed the boy's curly hair.

Lauren said, "He always like that."

"Like what?" asked Zora.

"Playing—getting in trouble. Touching things."

"Why don't both of you children go out back—" Zora pointed toward the door to the back room. That door opened to my washroom where I put the washtubs up on planks cross some hosses. Zora say it used to be the church office when the peoples fore us had the church but she and Kimball didn't need no office cept in her own bedroom which was plenty big enough for every kind of piece of paper they was gone need to keep a eye on. You had to go through there to get to the door to the backyard.

"Momma, show them the backyard, honey. Please. My nerves are bad. I'm sorry, Scoop."

"Come on, yall," I said, taking they hands. "Come on—"

And as I led them round the side of the pulpit to the back I heard Zora said to Scoop, "We going to take good care of them. They are in God's care now. This is the house of the Lord. We live a clean life here and we will make them clean."

2

I wanted to get the wash hung up fore the sun got too low. Juneboy and Lauren was with me in the laundry room, helping. When

I finished washing a shirt or whatever I passed it on to Lauren and
she jiggled it round in the rinse-tub then squeezed it much as she
could with her little bitty hands then lifted it — dripping on the new
linoleum — over to Juneboy. Juneboy bounched it round and round
in his tub — the last water stop. I got this sembly line set up, you
see, so I could wash a few things at my end, then go to the other
end of the line and take the things from Juneboy and give them
a big squeeze fore dropping them in the big straw basket on the
floor by his leg.

I hadn't seed them in over a month so there was plenty to talk
about. I was powerful worried bout these babies. So, while we
worked, I come just a trying to find out what I could.

"Yall hear from your momma?"

They both said yes ma'am.

"What she say?"

"She's fine."

"She say when she gon send for you?"

"No," said Lauren.

"Yes, she did," said Juneboy.

I figured Lauren knowed better what was in the letter since she
had a hand for words and could spell in her head. She always had
less trouble with the Bible than Juneboy. So, I said, "What else
she say other than being fine?"

"She moved to a new house," said Lauren.

"One with glass floors and silk walls."

"She say that in the letter?"

"Yes ma'am."

There wont no point in getting Juneboy's magination going no
ways further so I changed the subject.

I said, "Yall been reading the Bible and going to church like I
told you?" I looked over at they little faces and saw guilt.

They didn't answer.

"Well, it ain't your fault. Scoop should be shame of hisself. We
gon have to get you babies *saved* while you here."

"Will we stay here forever, Big Momma?"

"Do you want to stay?"

They didn't say nothing. So I let it go.

"Yall go down to the restaurant every day?"

"Yes ma'am."

"That's a sin, a awful sin," I said, feeling powerful angry at my son for his way of life. "That whole Decatur area one of these days will be struck off the face of the earth by the wrath of the All Mighty." I couldn't help myself. I had in my mind this picture, you see, of these trifling Negroes leaning around on the lightposts up and down Decatur and over on Butler. The smells of they fried fish and chicken and that sinful music from the bars bout sinning and all them pawnshops and poolhalls and beauty parlors with them old no good, sinning, nappyheaded womenfolk, and all them no count mens in the beer-taverns cussing and raising cane.

"Scoop don't take yall in to them houses of sin do he?"

They didn't say nothing. Maybe they didn't know zackly what a house of sin was even if they been inside one.

"Daddy took me to the barbershop yesterday," Juneboy said.

I looked around his ears. He had done had a haircut for sho but I never paid no tention fore he said it. "The one on Gilmer?"

"Yes, ma'am."

I knowed that place. That was where Scoop took me one time to innerduce the mens to his mother. They was a bunch of polite grinning fools. All sinners through and through! Not a one of them been inside a church since they was little. They looked that way cause they knowed I was a preacher-woman too — a woman of God.

I went over to Juneboy and rung out some wet clothes and dropped them in the basket.

I could hear Zora up in the church just starting to play the piano. She always had a ear for the piano. We got a girl come in on Saturday night and Sunday all day and Sunday night who plays. Her name's Betsy Mae.

"Let's go out now and hang up what we got done," I said, picking up the basket.

"Yes ma'am."

They took turns handing up wet clothes and towels to me while I pinned them on the lines. I had the pins in my little cloth satchel round my waist. I was humming,

> *Oh, just a little talk with Jesus*
> *makes everything all right;*
> *Oh, just a little talk with Jesus*
> *makes everything all right . . .*

Lauren had that worried look on her face. "If these not your clothes, Big Momma, then whose is they?"

"White lady name Miss Flannery Kitchens."

"That's a silly name," said Juneboy.

"Don't call nobody's name silly, Juneboy. She's a fine, fine lady — of one of the old, old families of Athens. She do a lot to help the colored peoples. Her granddaddy owned a plantation in the old days and freed all his slaves fore he had to do it. The slaves bought shares and farmed the land and owned it theyselves fore the end of slavery. That didn't happen much anywhere. Her grandmomma took a few of her slaves to England and got them educated over there and left them to live in London town where London Bridge and Big Ben is. These slaves became Englishmen and Englishladies. Miss Flannery's money built a Negro college down in Athens."

But they wont listening to me. I could tell.

Juneboy said, "How come she got so many clothes?"

"Cause she got a big family — daughter, son-in-law, they three children and one great-grand child by the oldest grandson."

"They live in a big house?"

"Sho do."

Juneboy scrunched up his nose. "How come you and Aunt Zora live in a church?"

His question surprised me. "Cause we holy people." Somehow that didn't sound like enough of an answer. I said, "Besides, the bedrooms ain't part of the church no how."

"Where we gon sleep?" asked Lauren. She dropped a balled-up shirt on the grass then gave me a look like she expected to hear bout it then picked it up and handed it to me.

"You gon sleep with me and Juneboy with the Reverend up front in his room."

"Big Momma," said Juneboy, "how old are you?"

I laughed. "Sometimes I feel like I must be a hundred or more. They say I was born round eighteen-and-eighty-two. So you figure it out. This is nineteen-forty-seven. You know how old that makes me?"

"I do," said Lauren, "I do —"

"No you don't," said Juneboy.

They went on like this for awhile then Lauren said, "I figured it out, Big Momma, I know, I know. It makes you be sixty-five years old."

I kissed the top of the child's head. I couldn't a done that kind of figuring in my head by myself. "You *so* smart. You gon grow up to be a scientist. Mark my words."

"What am I gon grow up to be, Big Momma?"

"You'll be a preacherman, like Reverend Hunter."

3

Zora woke me Saturday morning fore daybreak, said, "Momma, I think we should save the children fore tonight, fore the service starts." It tooks me some time to figure what the child was talking bout. When I did I sat myself up and reached over and got my teeths out of the waterglass. I put them in. I ain't shamed in front of Zora.

"This morning?" I thought, maybe Zora done gone off in the head again. (She did spend a long time in the crazyhouse back when she was running wild, fore she found God.)

"Yes. The way I figure it, Momma, there's no better time than to get them standing up for the Lord before they is fully awake. That way the purity of heart shines through before they can even stop to let the Devil in. You see what I mean?"

I did not see what she meaned. But then I never pretended to understand my oldest girl-child. She got away from me early in life and I lost touch with her. By the time she came back, just five or six years ago, she had God and I had God and God was the touching ground betwixt us. All I knowed about Zora was her love for God. And I had to trust that love. So I said, "If it's the Lord's will."

"Trust me, Momma. If we wait till tonight, something might go wrong and they could ruin the service. The Devil could be too strong. We better not take no chances."

"All right, dear."

Lauren had already moved. We could see she was waking up cause of our talking.

Zora said, "Lauren? You wake? Get up, honey."

"Ma'am?" Lauren turned over and rubbed her eyes.

"Get up, honey. We gone save you this morning."

"Ma'am?"

"Just get up. It's time to get up."

Zora sent me in to get Juneboy while she dressed Lauren. I tapped lightly at the Reverend's door. They was still sleep. Not a sound in there. I stood there not knowing what else to do. Then I thought, Zora should be the one to go into her own husband's bedroom, not me.

I went back to my bedroom and told her.

I finished dressing Lauren and Zora went up there and brought Juneboy back. She had his pants and shirt in her hand. He stood there in his pajamas rubbing his eyes. Zora told him, "You get yourself dressed, young man."

"Where're my clothes?"

"Right here." She handed them to him.

"Where're we going, Big Momma?" Juneboy asked.

"Never you mind," said Zora. "Just get yourself into your clothes. You'll see soon enough."

I finished Lauren then helped Juneboy into his pants. I was wondering how Zora and me was gone drive the Devil out of them without waking the Reverend.

We pushed them ahead of us into the church. It was cold and dark in there. Zora went over by the piano and got a box of matches. She struck one and lighted the candle on top of the piano. It showed us the room.

Zora said, "We're going to do them together."

"Do what?" asked Juneboy.

Zora took him by the shoulder and said, "You're going to pray to the Lord and ask to be delivered, to be freed of your sins. We're going to get you—both of you—to come to the Lord, to become pure in your heart, so you can dwell in his Kingdom forever, untroubled." She smiled at him nicely. "Don't that sound wonderful?"

"Yes ma'am."

"Okay, both of you kneel down here at the altar with Big Momma and me. We're going to pray together."

We all got on our knees.

"Dear Lord, God All Mighty," Zora said, "visit your spirit in the bosoms of these two children, cleanse out their souls, make them shine pure as your light—"

I started too, saying, "Lord, bring them the message of Jeremiah, the cleansing message, clean them of their sins, forgive them their transgressions—"

"Lift them up," Zora was saying, "lift them high, O Lord, high into your element of pure light—"

"Let them be there with you on Judgement Day, Dear Lord, and with you in your Resurrection—"

Zora had weeping in her voice. "Sad, sad is the condition of humanity, O Lord—"

"So sad—"

Zora started to groan something powerful. "Sinnnnnnnnnful, O Lord, *sin*ful is the condition of humanity. Save these babies from the warped life of humanity. Teach them while they are young to walk in the path of righteousness, for your name's sake."

I was singing too, "Cleanse them, O Lord, cleanse them in your blood, cleanse them, O Lord, pardon them, O Lord. Let them behold your presence, as the Lamb of God. Forgive them their innocence, deliver them, my God—"

Me and Zora went on like this, praying for the righteousness of the children, hoping for a sign, anything, from them, that the Lord had reached into the hearts and souls and touched them. Then I come justa hearing Juneboy crying up a storm and the po boy was shaking all over and I knowed by the way he was all out of control of his own body that the Lord had entered into him. But Lauren wont making a sound. She was just there on her knees with her forehead pressed ginst her hands like she was praying hard for it to happen to her too but she wont being touched.

We musta prayed that morning for over a hour. Lauren never did break down but I am sho we drove the Devil out of Juneboy.

4

The children stayed with us only about two weeks fore Scoop came and took them away, back to his own old sinful life. All the good work me and Zora did on them was undid by that rascal son of mine.

Then it musta been three months somewhere down the road of time after they was put on the train and set back up to Chicago to they momma, Ester. I member she wrote me a letter. Broke my heart, but I still got it. I keep it back there in the dresser drawer with my other portant papers.

This what Ester wrote —

Dear Miss Clardia,

Thank you for your letter about the life you say Adam and Lauren was living with their father. Although I know you mean well, Miss Clardia, I cannot help believe that you exaggerate. I remember too well some of the stories you used to tell when Lauren was only a infant and Adam was not yet walking, back when Scoop and me was still together in that shack of a house in Five Points where you used to come and babysit for us.

I can not find it in my self to believe that all the things you say happened really happened. They was down there a total of two months — July and August — and it would have to take two centuries to be exposed to the amount of sin you described in your long letter. I do not believe that Scoop ever let the children see him drunk or that he brought prostitutes into the house and had sex with them in front of the children or that he had his gambling friends in the house.

I have questioned my son and daughter carefully and am fully convinced that — when they say none of them things happened — they are not lying to me. Why should they? They have no reasons. If you are lying, I can't imagine why. I know you are a woman of God, so I think that you must not be lying on purpose but somehow you just got the wrong impression. You did not say in your letter how you got this information. You only hinted that a "little bird" told you so. Well, I don't know nothing about no little bird being able to talk. If you can't tell me who told you these lies, how do you expect me to believe you, in the first place?

I hope you will find it in your heart to understand how I feel and why I must take the stand that I take and disagree with you with all of my heart. I know we never got along well but at least now that Scoop and me are divorced and the past is the past maybe you could try to be more understanding.

I know you have the children's best interest at heart but you do not do them any good when you write a letter like that to me.

Sincerely yours,
Ester

Now, what do you think of that? I never was so hurt in all my life. I cried till my eyes was sore. I prayed, too. I only meant to do what was right.

Ten Pecan Pies

W ARM DECEMBER MORNING LIGHT and shadow moved evenly on Chickamauga. There were a few small clouds. The pecan trees alongside the farmhouse facing the highway were majestic. They moved their limbs gently in the breeze.

At another time the four children, Gal, Grew, B. B., and Moses, had taken two heavy, full burlap bags of pecans— gathered from the ground around the pecan trees—in to their grandfather, Grady Flower, and left them near him where he sat, pale and bent and paralyzed, in his silver wheelchair.

Even earlier, before their grandmother, Thursday Flower, sent them to gather the smooth, oval nuts, Grady had insisted on having them all brought into his room, because, he said, he wanted to *see* 'em.

Nobody suspected what he really had in mind. Certainly he knew Thursday was planning to bake ten pecan pies. She'd talked about it enough and the children walked around smacking their lips on the imaginary richness of the pies, saying *yum yum*.

At one point while the boys were shaking the pecan trees, Thursday's black, bony face poked from a window. "You get down outa that tree, Moses, 'fore you fall and break your neck! Let Grew and B. B. swing them limbs. You too little to be up there—stay on the ground and help your sister pick 'em up!"

Now Grady had had the ten pecans in his room hoarding them for a long time. Wouldn't even let the kids sample one. And Thursday herself had tried to approach the burlap bags only once days ago but Grady turned her back with his hickory walking cane. Yet Thursday had not given up. She needed pecans for the pies and the pies were for Christmas presents. And Christmas was tomorrow.

Thursday knew Grady pretty well and figured he'd give in. It was just a matter of time. It was still early morning and in time, sometime today, Grady would come around to seeing things her way.

Meanwhile, the boys were going to the woods shortly to get a tree. After that, Gal would help them cut paper decorations. Thursday had already shown them how. After supper, the children would crack pecans and she could start the pies and the opossum and the rabbits, which her son, Slick John, would come later to kill. At that time he would also help the boys erect the tree in Grady's room. Bring a little warmth and cheer to the old man. No need to always have the tree in the front. Last year Grady never even saw the tree. Refused to leave his room the whole week from Christmas to New Year's Day. Not that *that* was so unusual: there were months and years when he saw nothing beyond his own bedroom in this huge house built by his own hands. Anyway, Thursday would bake some beans. Greens and peas, which she preferred, were scarce this time of year. She'd make plenty of cornbread loaded with crackling. She'd unpack the dry figs and place them in bowls tomorrow. There would be peanuts and oranges sent by her daughters.

Thursday left the kitchen window. She went up through the large dark, cool house, up the back hallway, through the dining room, halfway up the front hallway, and turned into Grady's musty room. Grady was sitting before the blazing fire with a blue wool blanket over his legs. The orange light from the fireplace made his white hair seem pink. His head was hanging forward. Yes, he's asleep. Beyond him were the two bags of nuts. Grady's bed was directly behind him. Crossing in front of him and the fireplace was the only way to the burlap bags. Thursday stood there, a few inches from him, trying to weigh the moral quality of what she was tempted to do.

If she simply took the nuts she'd have to listen for days to his rage and hatred. But then she had to listen to his anger all the time

anyway. He hated her plenty and she knew he would never forgive her, first, for having had a lover years ago, and second, for
her good health. So why not take the pecans and make the pies
and hope for the best? How would God judge her deed? Was the
Devil telling her to do this? Though she was no longer a sinner,
at times when she felt herself giving in to the Devil's prodding,
she'd smile to herself. The Lord will forgive because it's not for
myself and it is to make others happy.

She tipped past Grady. One in each hand, Thursday started
dragging the bags out of their corner. They were too heavy to lift.
Stepping backwards, something hard touched her rear. She
stopped. Turned. Grady was holding out his walking cane to stop
her. "What you think you doing, woman?"

"These are the pecans, ain't they? I'm going to bake some pies.
I *told* you, Grady." She let the bags rest against each other.

"I planted them damn pecan trees over thirty years ago!" he
yelled. "They're *mine*!" His eyes bulged. Spit hung from his tooth-
less mouth.

"Yes, but my God, Grady, you can't *eat* 'em all!" From her long
skinny hands she wiped pecan dust on her red and white checker-
board apron. She stood there looking at her broken husband and
smelling the decay of his body. She tried to keep him clean but
it wasn't an easy task. His white shirt had yellow stains every
morning after coffee. Sometime he'd wet his pants. Now, almost
instinctively, while she spoke, she looked to see if he was dry. He
was.

"*My* pecans," he mumbled. Sheepishly, he looked at the flames.

She sensed she was going to win him over now. "*Lord*! I don't
know what to say! Grady, sometime I think you done lost your
mind. You act like you done lost your mind. You act like you
touched in the head. The way you carry on is a shame!" She
stopped and reflected on what she'd said. The tone was the important element. It had been gentle and compassionate. She had to
make him feel the proper amount of shame without making him
angrier.

She waited a few minutes for him to respond but he said nothing. He continued to hang his head. She left the bags where they
were, out of place—closer to his chair actually, and she walked

away. At his doorway she turned and saw him poking, with his smooth walking cane, at the tops of the burlap bags, trying to cover the nuts. Soon now he'd have a change of heart.

In the kitchen she began washing the sweet potatoes and humming to herself. As the dirt fell away their dark earth red color emerged. In any mood singing was natural. Thursday's lips began to move.

> *O, sinner man what you gonna do,*
> *O, sinner man what you gonna do,*
> *O, sinner man what you gonna do,*
> *on Judgment Day?*

The wooden bucket in which she worked was situated on a bench beneath one of the four kitchen windows. Beyond this window, at the edge of the yard Thursday could see her youngest grandchild, little Gal, with pigtails and in a blue cotton dress, feeding the fat opossum through the hole in the top of his makeshift box in which he'd been kept now for seven weeks. The box was on short stilts. There were two other wooden boxes arranged the same way, with one side of each made of screen, and with the hole in the top. In each of these was a fat rabbit. The opossum was black and grey. The rabbits were brown and white. When Gal finished feeding the opossum she patiently stuffed carrots and corn and breadcrumbs, the same stuff she'd fed the prehensile-tailed creature, into the rabbit boxes. The wild animals had been caught by the boys in traps set in the woods. And, along with her usual duty of feeding the chickens, Thursday had assigned Gal to the task of fattening these restless animals for slaughter and ultimately for the delight of the holiday season. Watching the little girl Thursday was aware that Gal had become attached to the animals and this was bad.

Apparently Gal had already recently fed the chickens because Thursday would hear the hens in the yard making a fuss over the feed. And the rooster grumbling. It was midday and this was the second feeding. Slick John would not come until five or six. By then, maybe Grady would give up the pecans. Thursday now remembered she had earlier sent Moses to the cellar, a damp dark musty place beneath the house, to get more sweet potatoes. What was he doing down there? Loafing? And B. B. was taking an awful long time to feed the hogs. By now he should be bringing in the wood Grew was chopping out near the fig tree. She could hear the ax screeching in the wood each time it struck.

Soon the boys finished their chores and went off to the woods for the tree. Grew carried on his shoulder the long, two-handled saw and B. B. and Moses carried the ropes. Though it was early afternoon the ground and undergrowth and bushes were still slightly damp from the night because the sunlight this time of year was not very powerful. They went single file deep into the forest, searching for and reexamining trees they had already tentatively selected. It had to be the very best evergreen they could find. It should be straight and tall and noble. It would be a thing they'd erect in the house and it had to have the finest qualities possible. They stopped, reconsidered and rejected several before they found the right one—one they had not previously seen—at the edge of the canyon where the Indians used to commit suicide. When they saw it they each knew it and there was no need to say anything.

But they had to be careful. This prince of an evergreen was right on the very edge and if it were cut down the wrong way they'd lose it in the canyon. B. B. worked at one end of the saw and Grew at the other. Moses, pulling on a rope tied—by lanky Grew—midway of the sturdy tree, desperately tried to direct the way it would fall; and if he were successful, this meant he'd have to move pretty fast, since he was struggling with the rope right on the spot where the prize would fall.

The landing went well. Moses jumped to safety and right away they started roping in the limbs to make it easier to carry.

Still, it was not easy getting it out of the woods. The path was narrow and dense and there was no road that led to their place.

When they arrived at the edge of the backyard they saw their Uncle Slick John wiping his hands on an old rag. His hands and clothes were bloody. Near him, spread out on the grass, were the slaughtered opossum and the two rabbits. Standing near the hedges nearby was Gal, sobbing. She continued to cry with her thumb in her mouth and she kept her eyes closed. The boys put down the trees to rest. They stood watching. A white hen was standing on the edge of the huge black kettle in which Thursday made lye soap. The rest of the chickens had gone away in fear of the killing and were now scurrying around the far side of the fig tree and grapevine on stilts at the left side of the house.

Thursday stood on the back porch with a pan of water in her hands. She, too, was silently watching.

Slick, a little drunk as usual, smelling of cheap moonshine, finished cleaning his hands and went over to Gal. He squatted before her. She was his favorite. He took her in his big dirty arms. "Honey, don't you know people have to eat? It don't mean we don't like the animals. We just have to eat. They eat. You see they kill each other to eat. And besides, tomorrow is Christmas. Don't you want to have a happy Christmas dinner?"

She did not answer but Slick John gently rocked her little body in his arms. A bubble of snot formed at the tip of her nose. And she laughed when it popped.

Hearing her laugh, Slick said, "Thata girl."

The boys picked up the tree and brought it up into the yard and let it down again at the steps. They did not want to watch Slick John pet Gal. He never showed them any sort of affection.

Slick went over and looked at the tree. "Pretty fine tree. Y'all getting to be experts." He smiled. "I'll help you put it up."

After the tree stood erect in Grady's room, Thursday asked Slick John to try to talk to Grady about the pecans. And he said he would try.

But it didn't work. Thursday waited in the hallway. Slick John came out. "He won't give 'em up, Ma. Just be patient with him. You know Pa."

Sure, she knew Pa all right.

The evergreen smelled good in the house. Slick John left, to go home to his wife, Lucy. The children sat on the floor cutting out red blue green yellow silver gold purple and orange paper strips circles triangles stars diamonds loops and bells to decorate the tree. Its odor mingled with the cooking smells coming from the kitchen. Though they'd had supper already the aroma of the Christmas food pervading the house made them imagine they were hungry again. The pungent smells of baked sweet potatoes, beans, and wild meat, swam in torrents throughout the house and beyond. As they used their blunt scissors they chattered away about the glory of tomorrow.

They were on the floor near the tree. Grady was in front of the fireplace. The fire was weak, it needed wood. As the children talked among themselves, Thursday stood in the doorway behind them. They were unaware of her presence until she spoke. "Tomorrow is going to be a big heartbreak if your grandpa don't give us the pecans." She said it loud enough for the old man to hear.

They looked up at her face. But she was looking at her husband there across the room.

She went over to his side and touched him.

"Grady." Her voice was low and smooth but firm. "The pecans was for the pies. It's not like I'm asking you for something for *my-self*. You may hate me but this is wrong. Lord knows you're wrong. I want to give our son and his wife two pies. And Mr. Hain Alcock. And Apostle Moskrey. I want to send some to our daughters, too. And old folks who are alone out on Remus Road. Them people don't have nobody who care about them. They could just as well be dead. I figure the least I could do is give them a nice pecan pie on Christmas day. I was going to take them over there myself. . . . "

Grady was pretending he hadn't heard. He looked at her quickly then looked away nervously at the burlap bags. Then, at the flames jumping in the fireplace.

"You know that set of books the judge gave you for Christmas when you was a little boy? Well, I was thinking about them today. They still in that closet over there and I know they must have made you pretty happy. You kept them all these years. Took 'em with you to architecture school. They meant something to you. I know a pie ain't important as books but a person living alone with nobody might really be thankful to get one. Just like you was about the books."

He looked again at Thursday.

The children snickered.

"Thursday," he murmured, "what you waiting for? The pecans over here in the corner." He touched the bags with his cane, quickly and lightly, a magician about to make magic. "By the time you get to 'em they'll be rotted away."

Thursday suddenly kissed the side of his face. The first time in years. The old man hardly knew how to react. He blushed. He took a deep breath and spoke. "Now, would you give me my pipe—and take these dusty bags outa my way . . . ?"

Already the children were laughing. Gal clapped her hands together and shrieked. "Grandma kissed Grandpa!"

Thursday gave him his pipe and lit it for him and he smoked it with enjoyment. Grew and B. B. helped her drag the bags of nuts into the kitchen.

After Thursday helped Grady to bed the children soon finished decorating the tree and went with her to the kitchen to crack nuts. The four of them, up past their bedtime, sat around the table using the nutcrackers—home-made gadgets. Some of the sweet oily kernels they popped into their mouths and ate. Meanwhile, Thursday worked skillfully with the eggs and butter, the vanilla and pecans she kept taking from a pile on the table. While the children cracked nuts she beat more eggs and mixed more butter. The huge black stove continued to roar. Once in a while Grew added a piece of wood to its fire. Thursday started humming and soon was singing.

> *Two big hosses hitched to a slide,*
> *Me and my Jesus gonna take a ride.*

And the children joined her, remembering the song from church. But as they sang they kept their voices low so as not to wake Grady.

Before long Gal fell asleep with her face on the table and pretty soon Moses could not keep his eyes open either. He kept nodding. Grew and B. B. kept breaking the smooth-shelled nuts and occasionally eating the tasty kernels.

Finally, though, even Grew and B. B. gave in to sleepiness and Thursday said, "Y'all better go to bed." It was already past midnight.

Once the boys were asleep in their beds in their room and Gal asleep in Thursday's bed, Thursday returned to the kitchen and finished baking the pies. The children had supplied enough pecans. And she worked with the patience of a miller until the rooster crowed and daylight turned at the edges of the windows where the old green shades never fully covered them. Now, once the rooster started he kept up his arrogant sound for over an hour.

Thursday finished the ten pies and the wild meat and the vegetables and placed them on the large table to cool. She dumped a little water on the fire in the pit of the stove. It made a sizzling sound and stopped suddenly. Yet the warmth stayed.

II

The Exchange

"There are some secrets which do not
permit themselves to be told."

—Edgar Allen Poe,
"The Man of the Crowd"

I'M A SECRETIVE MAN. I've learned the hard way to be careful about what I do and say. Trouble taught me this. Although I attempt to avoid trouble, I've discovered that it is not entirely possible. Learning this took years, I'm embarrassed to say.

When I decided to exchange teaching posts with another professor on the other end of the country in which I was born and in which I remain a citizen, I had the hardest example of my own inability to reduce disorder to an acceptable level. The initial idea of exchanging was his.

The other professor, who shall remain nameless, taught a rather strange version of the same subject I teach at my university on normal occasions. He described in detail his approach. He was enthusiastic but fearful that my university might not approve of his method. I quickly reassured him of the department's flexibility.

In his trickle of letters, my potential exchangee presented himself as a "laid back" person who had learned to accept the calamities of life. Well, I said to my wife, this exchange should be pleasant. I had heard from my colleagues that exchanges could turn out to be nightmares. This would be my first. Judging from his letters, I could not have hoped for a more understanding person with whom to trade.

It took six months' worth of correspondence to set up the transfer. I negotiated with our course committee and won its endorsement on what my substitute would teach. I told him everything I

37

could think of about our house: it's advantages and shortcomings. I drew up a long list of telephone numbers and addresses of local merchants I thought the best or most dependable along with the names and numbers of repair services. I told him exactly what to do in emergencies, gave him our doctor's name and address and told our doctor about my exchangee, his wife and son. My wife arranged for the boy to be enrolled in the neighborhood high school. He was fifteen. Let's see. What else? God, I can't remember everything but I do remember my wife and I thought they deserved the best care we could give.

All during the six months before the exchange, I wrote to him two or three times a week—about the house, the school, insurance, the mail service, garbage pickup, the yard, lawn, helpful neighbors. In the whole time I got, in return, maybe one third as many letters from him. Well, I thought, he's busier than I plus no doubt more efficient and better organized and therefore in no need of having to write so often.

As I said, he lived on one coast and I on the other. My end was warmer than his. This fact brought us to consider the practicality of also exchanging cars. His was better suited for mountains (of which there were plenty in his area) and mine was a fair-weather one. The question was resolved quickly: we would leave our cars at home where they functioned best. The minute the decision to swap cars was made I phoned my car insurance guy and made the necessary adjustment. Then I quickly sent word that all was well on my end where the car was concerned, assuring him that he would be covered while driving. Three weeks later he responded saying he hadn't gotten around yet to seeing his guy. I waited. Finally, after two more weeks he sent a hasty note saying he had made the insurance arrangements. His car, he assured me, although two years older than mine, was in excellent condition.

My wife and I continued to work hard to get the house in the best possible shape. We replaced the worn carpet in the hall, repaired some of the siding on the windward side of the house. On the kitchen floor where the tile was cracked we placed new squares, had our neighbor the plumber install a new drain-pipe under the kitchen sink because the old one leaked. We also de-personalized the house by taking away our most personal objects — such as family pictures — and storing them in the shed out back. In this way, they could claim the space better.

When there was only a week to go before the actual move was to take place, he wrote with the distressing news that his department still had not approved what I had requested to teach. Five months earlier, I had been led to believe otherwise. Thinking all was settled concerning the four courses, I had spent many hours preparing my materials and now had no time to junk those plans and start all over again. I telephoned him — in distress — but there was no response. In a few hours I tried again, and by then my anger was somewhat under control. When his wife got him to the phone he stammered an apology and told me that, although the titles of the courses were now different that I should not hesitate to use the same materials I had already worked up. Nobody, he said, would know the difference. Thanks a lot, I thought. Well, they wouldn't quite fit but I figured I could bend them a bit.

Then the time came.

We left the keys with a neighbor and took a taxi to the bus station then the bus to the airport. Once my wife and I were buckled into our seats on the airplane we agreed that there was nothing further we could do to make the exchangee and his family comfortable in our house. We'd left brochures for the furnace, the TV, the stove, the fridge, the record-player, along with a welcome note on the table. If there were problems each family was only a telephone call away. I took my wife's advice now and pushed my thoughts toward the coming adventure. We would enjoy the other coast and the mountains. I suddenly felt carefree and ordered a scotch on the rocks. My wife requested a Coca-Cola, as usual.

We knew where to look for the keys: under a loose plank on the porch. A plant in a flower pot would be sitting on the particular plank. We also had the name of the neighbor to the left who was friendly with them but I did not want to have to go asking questions or favors right away.

Our plane landed and we claimed our bags and after the hassle of getting out of the airport, got to the town by bus. At one point during the hour's ride I hugged my wife and kissed her cheek. She squeezed my hand and kissed her wedding ring.

The keys were indeed under the plank. The house had been described to me in an early letter. It looked far better than I had had any right to expect. It was ranch.

But the front door didn't work too well. You had to wiggle it from side to side till you disengaged the lock. I think, after I was exhausted, my wife got the damned door open after ten or fifteen minutes of jiggling the key.

With the door opened, we began taking our luggage in from the driveway where the taxi driver had dumped it. When this was done I took the car keys and went out to the driveway to take a look. Up close, it was muddy and rusted out along the fenders and the lower body — especially around the bottom of the doorframe. I got down and checked the tires. They were worn unevenly and badly.

I got in. It was a delight to find that the seatcovers were of cloth rather than that horrible plastic you see. I moved the seat closer to the wheel; tilted it a bit. While sitting there, I became aware that the entire dashboard was filthy with grease and dust and something else I have no name for. Then I saw the cracks in the plastic around the radio and the ashtray. I opened the glove compartment. It was stuffed with a jungle of things: a deck of cards, broken sunglasses, cassette tapes, a greasy rag, other things. I closed it back but it fell open again. I slammed it and it stayed. Then I put the key in and turned it just to listen to the motor. I had to turn the key ten times before the engine kicked in. When it did, the thing groaned as though in physical pain.

I went into the house. My wife was not immediately visible. I called out and she called back that she was in the kitchen. I found the kitchen by taking the direction from which her voice had come. I felt frustrated by my experience with the car and wanted to tell her what I had learned. But when I got to the kitchen, I found her sitting slumped in a chair at the table, looking very dejected. What was wrong? She told me to look at everything. Everything?

I looked around. I began to see what she was seeing. Beyond being in a kitchen that appeared to be normal, I found myself standing in an abnormally dirty kitchen. There were dirty dishes in the sink, jelly and butter smudges on the counter, dust on the tiled floor. My wife told me to take a look in the refrigerator. I didn't know if I wanted to. But I did. I opened the door and looked in. On first sight it seemed that every inch of space was crammed with stuff. Among the many, many things were a half-used carton of milk with an expired date, a topless plastic tub of butter with toast crumbs stuck here and there where a knife had stabbed, a moldy pack of bacon, an array of left-overs wrapped in aluminum paper. Behind me, I heard my wife tell me to take a look at the vegetable bin. I reached down and pulled it open. I saw two rotten heads of lettuce and three or four shrunken lemons with a stack of other things beneath which, at one time in the past, had been either green or yellow but were now all the same color of brown. I guess I shook my head in disbelief. I heard my wife begin to laugh at my bewilderment or out of frustration, I don't know which.

I closed the fridge door and turned back to my wife and reminded her that we were on an adventure. Besides, my exchangee and his family probably thought they were doing us a favor by leaving the thing full of fresh and delicious-looking food. Since there had been no welcome note anywhere in sight, perhaps this and the lived-in look of the rest of the kitchen was meant to be a kind of sincere, warm handshake.

Next, we explored the bedroom. There were family pictures on the dresser. The room itself was much smaller than I had been led to believe. I tested the mattress by pressing my hand on it to see how much resistance it could give. I was delighted to find a hardness necessary for my bad back. Meanwhile, my wife had opened the closet door and made a sound closely related to a scream. I turned to see her standing there with her hand over her mouth. Surely she was over-reacting to something. There couldn't be a dead body hanging in there! I went to see what was wrong. The closet was full of books! I couldn't believe it. (At home we had cleared out all three closets in anticipation of the exchange.) It wsan't even possible to force a shoe into that closet, let alone hang garments!

I dashed through the house to find the study where there was supposed to be another closet. There was. It was much smaller, but, thank God, almost empty.

We found the boy's room and opened the closet there. A huge

greasy boat motor had been placed on the floor on an opened
newspaper. I swore. My wife told me to calm down. She was
right. The space, she said, above the motor was free. There was
no reason why we couldn't hang clothes there. You just had to be
careful not to drop anything. Or move the motor? Well, this
whole trip was an adventure, and . . .

We fetched hamburgers and fries at a nearby fast-food place
and came back to the house. We ate and went to bed. All night
I tossed and kept myself and my wife awake.

I won't bore you with the details of disappointment we suffered
over the next three or four days. We were at the beginning of fall
and could still indulge our passion for hiking and do some week-
end camping before the cold weather came. We planned to discover those much-written-about mountains of the area! There was
a fireplace in the living room. There, in the freezing nights of winter, we could make love or read to each other. It was going to be
a very, very good adventure!

Then I met the people at the school.

First, the secretaries. I figured out pretty quickly that they had
a "slot" for me. I was the exchangee. This meant that I was temporary. In academia, when you are temporary, you are not necessarily treated well. If you are lucky you are treated with respect
if not care. There was trouble finding an office for me. They for-
got to give me a mailbox. When they apologized, I smiled and assured them that there was no problem. I was on an adventure.

Next, the professors. I met three or four in the mailroom. One
was extremely friendly and suggested we have lunch together one
of these days. Another said hi and welcome. There was no formal
reception for me (although on the other coast there was one for
my exchangee—I later learned).

Then classes started and I met the students. Aside from a girl
who was obviously having emotional problems, they were—as a
group—more serious-minded and hard-working than I could have
hoped for. Going to class became a stimulating challenge. Some
of them dreamed of careers; a few expressed a passion for philos-
ophy or art or physics. It was refreshing.

Meanwhile, my wife and I adjusted to the house and to the
car—despite problems. I refused to let them get me down. We put

the annoyances to the back of our minds. We hiked; we camped. We drove along the coast. We stopped in cozy little ocean-side restaurants where we ate fried oysters or squid. The mussels were good too.

We never wrote to my exchangee to complain about any of the problems we encountered living in his house and driving his car. We kept thinking: adventure, adventure!

In time, a few letters came from the exchangee—mainly when he had a complaint. I can't remember them all! For awhile they thought the stove had a faulty oven but it turned out she didn't know how to turn it on. Somebody broke into the shed and stole some of the things we had stored there. The exchangee bought a new lock. I thanked him. He said the weather was bad.

There were other complaints: students there had raised protest to his method of teaching; the Chair was cool toward him; his son hadn't made any friends; his wife had a cold; some driver had dented a fender of my car—but the insurance company covered the cost of fixing it good as new, he said.

Before we knew it, it was spring: shrubbery and trees in the front and back yards began to show signs of green. The last snow fell in the middle of April. We began to hike more and to camp on some weekends. One time we saw a huge bear walking upright through the trees. We stood still, holding our breath till he passed. We explored the coastal area, going farther up than we had in the fall. Now, my second semester was easier than the first and I liked the new students. Although my exchangee's car had cost us over three hundred dollars in repairs, we told ourselves things could have been worse.

The time to leave drew near. We spent a week at the end cleaning the exchangee's house—hopefully, not as a cynical statement. We were just in the habit of cleaning up after ourselves. My wife called a professional carpet cleaner who came out and did a fine job. We put new washers in all the faucets; replaced a broken glass and one cup. We left the refrigerator empty and clean as a whistle. There were no dirty dishes in the sink—of course!—and the counter was clean. The tiled floor was clean enough to eat on. When we arrived the bathroom seat cover had been loose: now we bought a new one. We probably over-did it a bit.

Then we called a taxi. It was a fine day in the middle of August as we were driven to the bus station and from there on to the airport. At one point I almost leaped into the air and clicked my heels but the weight of the luggage kept me in check.

On arriving home we found the door closed but not locked. It was mid-day and they had left the day before. I was furious! My wife gave me the look that said, Calm down — do you want an ulcer. She grew up in the country where people rarely lock doors; I, in the city, where only fools do not. One of the upstairs windows — I had noticed the minute we stepped out of the cab — was open and therefore also unlocked.

We went in. The house smelled bad — like dirty socks. With the door ajar, I began to bring in the bags. Meanwhile, my wife was already exploring the house. She came back to the hall holding her face. Her eyes were closed. She said the whole house was filthy. Well, I thought, she was probably exaggerating a bit.

I had to go to the bathroom. When I finished I noticed that the tub was dirty with grease and hair; the face-bowl contained a similar coating of the same sort of human waste. There were on the counter fingernail polish stains and a scattering of face powder. The mirror was cracked in the corner as though it had been hit with a tiny hammer.

On the way back to the front hall, I glanced into the bedroom and the study. The bedroom stank and the study had been rearranged for some reason. The carpet beneath my feet was filthy with God-knows-what!

I found my wife in the kitchen looking into the refrigerator. I went and looked over her shoulder. Every inch was stuffed with things. Among them, I noticed right away, a half-used carton of milk with an expired date, a topless plastic tub of butter with toast crumbs stuck here and there where a knife had stabbed, a moldy half-finished pack of bacon. I didn't want to see any more. I backed away and stepped on a dead mouse.

I was speechless. My wife turned and wept on my chest. I held her close. I proposed, in a soothing voice, that we go out to dinner then check into a motel and pretend we were just beginning to get to know each other. We would make love with the passion of those gripped by wonderment. Then watch the late movie—and it would be about a couple learning the mystery of love and how to trust it; and also about how they finally come to accept the problems they know are always coming. It would be a perfect family movie!

Marilyn

M ARILYN'S MOTHER CAME TO see her. Marilyn noticed right
away that her mother was drunk. Marilyn's mother
coughed blood into her handkerchief. The flag on the flagpole outside the window went up. It was seven in the morning.

"You're getting so high and mighty you can't even come to see
your own mother."

Marilyn was in no mood to fight. She started making coffee.

Marilyn and her boyfriend Peter have the place to themselves.
They are listening to blues records: Bessie Smith, Dinah
Washington, and Memphis Slim. Peter asks her about her mother.
Without answering she looks at him and decides not to make love
with him tonight.

Marilyn is dreaming of her mother. A dog is snapping at her
mother's legs. Her mother is scared. The dog pulls Marilyn's
mother's blue skirt off and Marilyn's mother is left standing there
in public in her slip. Now the dog loses interest in the skirt and
returns to snapping at Marilyn's mother's legs.

Marilyn's mother is leaving Marilyn's apartment. She is
slightly drunk. She is a pathetic shabby woman whose eyes are
narrow red slits. Her breathing is laborious.

Marilyn is alone, crying. She is lying across her bed. Her shoulders lift and fall with her sobbing. It feels good to cry like this in the warm darkness of her apartment. The bed feels good. The hum of the refrigerator in the kitchen has worked its mechanical rhythm into her system. "My sadness," Marilyn says to herself, "even my sadness feels good."

Marilyn stepped off the pavement and went across the grass. It was dark. Out of the corners of her eyes she watched to see if she was being watched. She was in the clear and it was a warm summer night. After all it was nothing for a person, even a woman, a beautiful dark woman, to step off the sidewalk and enter the darkness of the park. People do it every minute on a hot night like this. She was almost talking to herself. Stop feeling guilty. She walked into a thicket of large trees and bushes and hid herself between two hedges. Now all she had to do was wait. Before long somebody would come this way.

Mother Visiting

B EFORE WE REALIZED IT we were in Little Italy. And we were exhausted so I grabbed a taxi. This was not Alta Vista. Mother was not young.

In Chinatown things had been different. My roommate and I took mother to a Chinese restaurant where we stuffed ourselves. Jessica is my roommate. She's from sunlight and now lives in my shadow. We are not impassioned.

Mother's visit would last only three days.

She was telling us again about the taxi driver who brought her from La Guardia. "He believes in Hitler. He said his ambition is to kill his mother and bury her out back. I asked him what she ever did to him. He said she gave birth to him and I said it serves you right you murderer you." At this point, like the previous time, she laughed.

We went to a Turkish restaurant. A Turkish bellydancer danced for me. I fell in love with her. Jessica, who is also beautiful and a great dancer, was amused. Mother started telling us the rest of the taxi driver's agony. I said, "He's definitely not Upper West Side, not Morningside; sounds like Queens or Bronx."

Mother goes to the window and looks out at the dirty street. "The street is dirty," she says with a sadness I have not heard in her voice since my father stood in the doorway ready to go away to war. Before Jessica and I realized it mother was saying the same thing again. And she never read Gertrude Stein.

Most of her life she had made her living as a dressmaker so naturally she was interested in dress shops. We went out onto the dirty street in search of a dress shop or several dress shops. Before we realized it we were in a dress shop in Chinatown then one in Little Italy. Mother told the dress shop keepers the story of the taxi driver who wants to kill his mother.

We windowshopped on MacDougal and Bleecker and on The Avenue of the Americas or Sixth Avenue. I was bored. Jessica spoke of sporting goods in connection with her plans to camp next month. She, too, was obviously bored with dresses. Jessica never wore dresses. She was a jeans girl. When Jessica dressed up she wore slacks from Nurnberg and hats from Dunnlop in Discovery, Maine. Her boots did not come from the North Eastern United States. They were imported from Zalon's Leather in Worley, Montana. My mother did not like Jessica. Secretly Jessica did not like my mother. But we were all nice to each other.

On the second night of mother's visit she had supper in Harlem with an old friend, Mrs. Velma Mae Thompson. Velma Mae Thompson was not an interesting person. I saw her once when I was a child. She was basically interested in cutting the risk of heart disease. She spoke often of the importance of a careful diet. She did not believe in medicine. Apparently she did believe in my mother.

With mother out of the house we played checkers and drank dark beer. We had more fun than the President.

Mother is sitting at the kitchen table sipping coffee and smoking her endless cigarette. A hundred and seventy-five old photographs are spread out on the table around her coffee cup. It is not surprising that she is interested in the good old days.

Jessica puts on a wide floppy hat and announces that she's going to therapy. Mother wants to know what is therapy. Jessica patiently gives mother a balanced overview of therapy. Mother still does not understand.

I returned alone to the bellydancer and asked her out. She said sure. We had dinner in Schindler's then went to Hufstader's for drinks. Then to her place where we spent three hours reading Edith Sitwell. I promise you the President himself never had such fun.

The next thing I knew it was time to go home.

The taxi driver came for mother. I walked down to the curb with her. Jessica waved from the window.

The taxi driver said, "I believe in Hitler, Miss. My ambition is to kill my mother and bury her out back. You will want to know what she ever did to me, right. Right. She gave birth to me that's what she did."

"Young man," said my mother, as she climbed into the cab on her way to the airport, "you are a disappointment!"

III

The Horror!

1

S HE WAS TAKING THE LESSONS because of her Intended. He loved scuba diving and by the time he came home from the Navy she would be good at it too. Besides, out here it was the thing to do.

To pay for her lessons she agreed to star in a horror movie. These things were always humiliating. But it would be her first leading role. The director told her she would be the first Black girl to get such a part.

The scuba diving instructor said there might be wild dogs so be careful. She liked him. His big belly, like her father's, was a comfort. She was glad she was placed in his group and not in one of the others. In the van she was sitting close beside him on the front seat. Suddenly lightning reached into the van as they pulled off Five into a narrow paved road; lightning like last night's on the sand down at Children's Beach in La Jolla. Rain too had hit like hammers. Just a shower everybody said. Down the beach the light went out in the guardhouse. She blinked. The air smelled of mollusks and the waves were piling high and breaking hard out there in the dark. The flames under the grill-rack were dying under the force of rain. A yellow-brown dogfish lay a few feet away in the scrap of a recent beach fire. She watched, from under the plastic

53

with the others, the last sea gulls going toward the last light which had already gone long before.

Now, five minutes into the road the paving ran out and they hit dirt and started to hear barking. The rain poured down even while late afternoon sun was still up there. Somebody said wild dogs. She thought they didn't sound exactly like dogs. Maybe coyotes. She'd seen them in the desert while driving to Borrego Springs. That was back when everything about Southern California was still fascinating to a girl from the South Side of Chicago. The unbelievable ocean that stretched all the way to the other end of the earth! Bigger cars, newer houses, brighter clothes! Balboa Park was a make-believe world! There was no need to drive up to L.A. for Hollywood or Disney!

The diving instructor stopped the van in front of the Oceanography mess hall. He reminded them not to eat too much. She disliked the way he shook his finger at them when he spoke. It was the first time he'd done this and the first thing she disliked about him. Still, he was the best instructor the school had. Everybody said so. This finger-shaking business was the sort of thing she expected from the horror movie director — who also had a lot of other bad habits such as barking sharply — not of her scuba diving instructor.

She got out with all the others and waited for the instructor to finish locking the van. He then came and led them up a path to a low, flat barracks-like building. They followed him inside.

The cafeteria was huge and there were about fifty tables and guys who were dressed like Marines were coming in from the buffet line with their trays and sitting down to eat. There was a silence in her held firmly against a flat surface with the texture of cold stone, as she stood there in line holding her tray.

The steak tasted like reinforced wood and the potatoes like latex. Far off in the hills, as they ate, the wild dogs were howling.

When they finished the sun was going down. The instructor got them all together outside the mess hall. She was a little surprised to hear him say the men would go there — he pointed — to that barracks and the women — he pointed again — there, to the one on the left. Remember, he said, up at four-thirty in the morning.

The women's barracks smelled like a wet dog. There were

women in fatigues already there. One met them at the door. "Are you broads TDY?" Because her brother had been in service she knew what TDY meant. She looked at the other women in her group and saw them looking at each other and at her. She told the woman in fatigues they were scuba diving students. Fatigues smirked and said, "From Scripps?"

She couldn't sleep. The dogs were howling all night. She figured the hills had to be close.

She was the first to get out of bed and was fully dressed by the time the other students were stretching and yawning.

It was five before they all got their act together and made it down to the coast. Sea gulls were gliding overhead inspecting the sand. They all got into gear. She was first into hers.

The instructor led them to the rafts on the pier. The guys helped him get them down onto the water. The water looked calm and the wind felt brisk. The sun was just coming up out of the mountains she could see from the corners of her eyes.

Just at this point a Jaguar — red as fresh blood — drove directly onto the beach and two guys she recognized as instructors from the school got out. They came over and it was pretty clear within minutes that they were going to help. One had the shakes.

They were divided into three groups. She got the one with the shakes and his belly was flat.

In her group, which was composed of three women and five men, she was the first to get her tank pumped. The instructor's hands shook as he pumped. He then checked her mouth gear to make sure she had it on properly — so she assumed. She waited and watched while he did the same to the others. The other instructors were also pumping and checking.

Down here on the shore she couldn't hear the dogs. Far off at the horizon the sky was a complex maze of damaged crops — like those her uncle used to suffer down south.

Then they were ready. She was the first to go down.

Deep down the water felt dense and colder than before. It was morning cold. The instructors had fluorescent lights on their helmets so they could see the students. She felt like she was before a camera making a movie. All around her, the anemones with phosphorus in them were a panorama of multi-colored fingers waving and turning. No, they were not fingers: they were little, hidden cameras!

2

The director told her all she had to do was pretend she didn't see the guy. He was white wearing a black mask. Just act natural, said the director.

It was just a movie. In movies you didn't have to come into contact with others — even those you touched. In this one the director wanted her to play a white girl. It would be easy for her, the director told her, since she was neither black nor white.

She was the Victim and the antagonist was her Attacker. Lights. Action. The director gave the cameraman the word. This was the beginning. She was in the kitchen.

She pretended she didn't see the guy.

Don't look at the camera. You are going to be his first victim. He knows this but you don't. Act natural. Your first sight of him is out of the corners of your eyes. The director is speaking patiently and paternally.

Actually, before she saw him she saw his camera. At first she thought it was a gun. It pointed at her from the edge of the window.

Okay. Show fear! Cover your mouth with both hands. That's good. Now, quickly but slowly (yes, you can manage both at the same time!) gain control of yourself; try to appear calm. It must be clear that you are about to fall apart but on the surface you appear to be quite cool.

When she looked the second time he was gone.

He came again the next morning and pointed the camera at her just as before.

Unlike the day before, today you are wearing only your panties and bra and high heels. When you see him this time, hold your heart as though you fear it might burst out of your chest and spill, like an egg, across the floor. You're still pretending you don't see him, but already you're beginning to enjoy being the object of his fascination. You stop washing dishes and unhook your bra. Through the window you can hear his camera clicking.

The next morning the mailman brings the mail. Through the front window you watch him leave. You go out then on the porch and take the mail out of the box.

One of the items is an eight by eleven manila envelope. You open it at the kitchen table. It is a picture of you at the kitchen sink in your bra and panties and heels. With a Magic Marker somebody has drawn a large black penis on the print. It points toward your rear end.

Now you know you're in for it. Any sensible person would surely call the police at this point. But you rather enjoy the danger, the mystery of it.

He didn't come the day the picture came. She was vaguely irritated all day. She watched soap operas and called her mother and her girl friends and made an appointment with the dentist. Opening her mouth for him had always given her some sort of perverse pleasure.

The director told her that it was the next morning or six months later. She was beginning not to trust the woman she was supposed to be, yet she needed the money: scuba diving lessons were expensive.

You are waking slowly, sensing the light and you hear a noise like somebody opening a window or a door. At the edge of your sleep you think it's the neighbor getting his newspaper from his front porch. You remember you heard it hit his door, as usual, about an hour — two hours? — ago.

But as you continue to wake you realize you hear somebody actually walking down the hallway in your apartment. He's coming toward your bedroom. You sit up, trembling. You hold your heart as though you fear it might leap from your chest.

The camera moved in closer and focused on her mouth, showing its interior: her teeth, her tongue, the roof of her mouth, as she screamed.

He's standing in the doorway of your bedroom. You're sitting up, white as a Nordic. Your knees are against your chest and you have the sea-green sheet clutched to your chest. You're still screaming. His face is black as night.

Your intruder remains motionless or appears to be.

In your screaming you begin to choke, as though under water drowning. Your screams give way to sounds of suffocation. The camera moves in on your bulging eyes.

You are broken, deep in the ocean and your submersion is totally unnoticed by any of the other scuba diving students. You are invisible as you sink.

3

The instructor focuses his light on her as she drifts down. She can see his concern. His eyes — behind the helmet-glass — are those of an alarmed person. She wants to reassure him but cannot find the right motion — the correct signal. Waving her arms as she does only gives the impression of distress.

When he reaches her, stopping her descent, she is relieved because she can see relief in his eyes. His helmet light shines above her face, up through the water pointing toward China.

He took her all the way up and the others followed. It was a clear April day but down the coast you could see clouds over Del Mar. Yet already the air was frigid with blinding light.

Her black rubber suit stuck to her like a second skin, especially now, out of the water. The rafts were bobbing in the water by the dock. The ocean breeze had a calculated thrust.

They sat on the beach for the follow-up lecture. This was better than watching sticks pointing to charts on walls in classrooms. She gazed at the horizon. She figured it must be nine or nine-thirty. She scanned the three instructors standing there — their backs to the ocean — minus headgear. The one with the gut was repeating the well-known safety rules. She felt guilty. But she knew she wasn't the only fuckup.

This time she was the only woman. Counting the instructor, there were four men. The phase-out in this program was rapid. This instructor was new to her. He had red hair. She liked him. His eyes were green with yellow specks. She'd once had a cat with eyes like his. "One time," he said, "a barracuda almost got us. I had my diving knife. The barracuda got attracted, I guess by the silver flash. He circled me, taking his time, just checking me out. That bugger kept circling the glint. I knew what was on his mind. When he lunged at my knife, I saw the huge mouth open, coming at me. I was fascinated by his magic. Yet I struck back and saw a stream of blood release itself from the corner of his mouth."

She squeezed her headgear between her knees. She closed herself against the image of a blade entering her.

The instructor refused to stop his story: "I was on shore. In a little while I saw the barracuda floating stomach-up on the surface. Like today, it was one of those fantastic blue days we get here in California. There was a good tide-wind so the heat wasn't heavy. I felt better than I'd ever felt in my life."

She listened to this and watched him without knowing what to think or feel.

He went on: "The barracuda's tail fluttered one last time before it gave in—like the legs of somebody being raped in an alley."

At this point, feeling the force coming up out of her, surging through her chest, she threw off her gear and staggered up to her feet, and began the difficult run across the sand, back to the road where the cars were shooting by like bullets.

Here, she stood waiting.

She was in an atmosphere of powdered sugar and unredeemable arrogance when her mother told her, from across the formica table, that the horror movie was now showing in the neighborhood theatre. As a mother she would never live down the shame. She chewed a French fry and licked the salt and grease from her fingers as her mother wept. For the first time she regretted bringing her mother out here from Chicago.

Reluctantly, she went to see the horror movie, to see for herself. Sitting in the dark theatre, waiting for the film to start, she smelled muskrats and wolves and thought she heard little animals scratching at baseboards and scurrying across the floor. Something bumped her leg. But maybe the smells were only the mold and rot in the walls. She was pretty sure the ticket girl hadn't recognized her. In fact, the girl hadn't even glanced at her as she pushed the ticket toward her across the silver metal surface.

The movie had been made in color but now, as it filled the

screen, she saw black and white. In the first few frames she saw herself in scuba diving gear, underwater, black as a rotten hambone, swimming against the suds of an endless whiteness. This didn't make sense: no such scene had ever been shot—not with her in it! Obviously somebody had pasted her onto the scene, made her move, kicking her feet and throwing her arms. She stood, ready to leave, but was unable to pull her eyes away. She sat down again and gave in to her own morbidity and anger.

One frame, showing her making ju-jitsu arm-swings—for no logical reason—ended with her surfacing. Behind her head sails furled. She imagined onyx, not black, not gray. On the horizon, a mainmast flew to pieces. Helmsmen ran along an embankment: the things going on in the background were more intense than the focused shot of her blazing eyes in the headgear. She began to get the idea that, if there was going to be a story, one of the helmsmen would turn out to be her Attacker.

This was still early in the movie. She has come up out of the water and has changed into street clothes—a sweater and jeans. She could amost hear the barking director directing her steps, the changing expressions on her face. Because of the light, she was transformed into a shimmering white figure drifting—as silent as a Venice gondola!—along the asphalt. She walked as though steered. In the sky above her, the moon and the sun were dying together in separate clouds. Below, at hip-level, behind her, sternposts and yardarms and ropes lifted in a string from washboards into high stays and planks. Sitting in the theatre watching herself, she was sure she smelled the fishiness of the scene. The camera followed her as she went past a yellow-lighted outdoor restaurant where Mexicans and Navajos and Anglos were eating fries and burgers and dogs and onion rings. An old Mexican beggar began to hobble along behind her. A pair of cops, swinging billysticks, passed in the other direction. Obviously, just her walking itself was supposed to be the subject matter: it was, presumably, interesting enough in itself to hold the viewer's attention.

She enters an unlighted street. She sees herself dark against gray. A couple of seconds into the scene, the camera focuses on the edge of a dark grey building. Fog hangs low and there is the

I hope you will find it in your heart to understand how I feel and why I must take the stand that I take and disagree with you with all of my heart. I know we never got along well but at least now that Scoop and me are divorced and the past is the past maybe you could try to be more understanding.

I know you have the children's best interest at heart but you do not do them any good when you write a letter like that to me.

Sincerely yours,
Ester

Now, what do you think of that? I never was so hurt in all my life. I cried till my eyes was sore. I prayed, too. I only meant to do what was right.

Ten Pecan Pies

WARM DECEMBER MORNING LIGHT and shadow moved evenly on Chickamauga. There were a few small clouds. The pecan trees alongside the farmhouse facing the highway were majestic. They moved their limbs gently in the breeze.

At another time the four children, Gal, Grew, B. B., and Moses, had taken two heavy, full burlap bags of pecans — gathered from the ground around the pecan trees — in to their grandfather, Grady Flower, and left them near him where he sat, pale and bent and paralyzed, in his silver wheelchair.

Even earlier, before their grandmother, Thursday Flower, sent them to gather the smooth, oval nuts, Grady had insisted on having them all brought into his room, because, he said, he wanted to *see* 'em.

Nobody suspected what he really had in mind. Certainly he knew Thursday was planning to bake ten pecan pies. She'd talked about it enough and the children walked around smacking their lips on the imaginary richness of the pies, saying *yum yum*.

At one point while the boys were shaking the pecan trees, Thursday's black, bony face poked from a window. "You get down outa that tree, Moses, 'fore you fall and break your neck! Let Grew and B. B. swing them limbs. You too little to be up there — stay on the ground and help your sister pick 'em up!"

Now Grady had had the pecans in his room hoarding them for a long time. Wouldn't even let the kids sample one. And Thursday herself had tried to approach the burlap bags only once days ago sense of warmth and dampness, the smell of tacos and popcorn. From the passageway between two buildings, a face glows in the shadows. It is the face of one of the helmsmen. He moves away from the center of the stark frame. In the next one, he peeks around the edge of the same building she saw a second before. As she continues, he appears, lurking in the shadows of each alley she passes. She can tell by the calmness of the self she sees on the screen that that self is unaware of the menacing presence of the helmsman.

Midway through, she sees herself cornered by wild dogs. She is in the crevice of two buildings, at the point where they join in a V-shape. It could be the Old World, the decay and mold—even in black and white—are so obvious. Just as they leap toward her throat the helmsman who has been following her steps into the scene and beats them off with a large stick.

She watches him rape her. The self up there fights till she has no energy left. In the scene she appears white, he black. The light keeps changing: she turns black, he white. Then he is spent. And she is sure now. She sees his face: he is the director himself.

She watches him lying there atop that other self. She feels the warm sweat and tender hardness of his belly and hears the concert of his breathing. She reflects on the fury of his grinding and pumping and speed, on his digging and agony and the explosion—and cries—of his humid pain. And she was very sure now: nothing, in the end, had come out of him, nothing except the fury and the pain. And another thing was equally clear: she has always known him and in all the centuries she has held him between her thighs, his frenzy has found its way into her nervous system and even into her blood.

Now, in the final frames, her trust of the image of herself moving, in tones of gray, before her on the large screen, lost more ground. She has torn away from the rapist, leaving much of her dignity and faith under his dirty fingernails. As she ran—along a beach that smelled of mollusks—a feeling she could not name crawled along the outer surface of her skin. Above the running figure of herself, a white sun in a black sky handcuffed the cloud that passed in front of it.

The movie hadn't been nearly as bad as she expected. She

walked home. She could hear the good-timers out on Ocean Beach yucking it up.

When she opened her door she immediately knew somebody else was in the room. She smelled him before she saw him. She heard him move and saw him at the same moment. He was in silhouette: a gray, quivering presence. She pushed the light switch. It was this or scream. The intruder was the scuba diving instructor, the one with the belly. Terror gave way to surprise and confusion. Through it all, she could hear the couple in the bungalow nextdoor fighting again about the adopted kid. He wanted to send "it" back and she wanted to keep "him." The instructor had an embarrassed look. With his hands behind his back, as she asked him why was he here, he took two steps in her direction. She held her right hand out like a traffic cop does when he wants to halt a line of cars. The instructor's face said in its grimness and weirdness that no light of compassion or wisdom ever burned in candlesticks made of pure gold and that all the fruit on every tree in the world was rotten and stank. He was a transformed person, no longer comparable to her father: a creature of self-loathing, contempt and torment. Poe might have put him in a story. She found his leer not only trying to enter her body but the sort of expression touched by some unknown evil alchemy. He grinned and his teeth showed. They were bigger than she remembered. She took a step back, and reached behind herself for the doorknob. It was there. The scuba diving instructor continued to advance on her, lifting his feet as though they were stuck in cement.

She opened the door. The zombie leered more furiously. She began to shake—felt herself shaking, losing confidence in her ability to escape. Physical pain moved in her lower intestines. The network of that same pain lifted up through her, like a bat, and circled her heart. The inner surface of her brains ached.

He was now only a few inches from her. He was wheezing. His eyes were those of a catatonic. Just as he said, "I saw the movie," she saw his hand coming. She stepped backwards through the door as he stepped up his approach. His hand, as though anticipating the feel of her breasts, spread like a Spanish fan.

Outside, she turned and ran down her walkway and across the sand—which was difficult and took a long while—to the black ocean. She could hear him coming, huffing and puffing, behind her.

She entered the water. The shock of the coldness exploded in her like being banged on the head with skis. The minute she hit, she realized her error. Should have run the other way — to the street, toward the hamburger and pizza lights. But maybe it wasn't too late. But it was.

He followed her down. While he was still struggling to get a firm hold on her, she lifted herself to him. He had taken off his pants and his stubby legs were moving like frog legs move in water. Feeling a confidence she had never before felt, she reached for his crotch and took a firm hold on his penis. She took it and its appendage into her mouth and brought her jaws together so hard she was sure she broke at least half of her teeth.

Letters

DEAR JULIE: I guess the thing about your letter that surprised me the most was the way you ended it. I mean with the word love. Somehow I didn't expect it and to see it was a surprise. But I know you meant it in a new sense, not the old sense we once thought we shared. But maybe even more a surprise than the word love was the letter itself. I guess I never expected to hear from you. Especially since you refused to talk to me when I called you in Jericho. And now you propose we become pen pals. Well I can say right now I'm not much for writing letters and never have been. Never had a pen pal. But I'm willing to try. I mean I will try to answer any letter you write and to let you know what I'm doing from time to time. But I'm not sure if it's worth it. If you know what I mean. In any case I am sure I can't tell you all my thoughts. I doubt if anybody can tell anybody all his thoughts. But I can tell you what has happened since we last met. Coming back here to New York was rough. At first. Especially having to stay in the same apartment me and Gail Smith shared. So I was determined to move. You will notice on the envelope my new address. I have a larger apartment and the neighborhood is nicer. I'm a bachelor again and beginning to like it. I have a new job I like very much. I'm Assistant Circulation Director of the new Black magazine for women, *Stance*. I'm sure you've seen it because it's everywhere in the nation on all newsstands. If you haven't seen it let me know and I'll send you a copy. It's a good magazine and we're proud of it and see a big future for it. I was in on the beginning of it. Along with the president and chief executive and the vice president I helped put together the proposal that got us our initial investors. And though there has been only one issue so far we have three in dummy on the drawing boards. We have problems of course but we have hope. Most of our problems at the moment have to do with personnel. So far most of the people we have employed have been good and willing to work for less than they could earn elsewhere. A few have caused serious trouble however. We had to let our editor-in-chief go last week and she was an absolute bitch about it. The following day we got a phone call from an unknown party telling us our building was about to go up in a blast. Naturally we called the police and they had us all clear out while they searched the place but they found no bomb. In my own department things are going well. We have good circulation. One of the biggest distributors in the country is handling *Stance*. Though in order to keep their service we have to maintain a certain standard. I suppose you're wondering how I, without a college education, managed to get into this line of work. Aside from luck it is the result of planning. A very good friend of mine, Jake Johnson, brought me into the initial group, knowing my talent for business affairs. Anyway this will give you a little idea of where my head is at lately. As for my personal life I have been trying to stay away from any serious involvement with anybody right now. I give all my energy to the magazine. I did see Gail two or three times about six weeks ago. It was a mistake. I think she hates me now. I ran into her one day just as she was coming out of the telephone building where she works. I wanted her to sit down with me in a nearby restaurant and have coffee and talk. But she refused. So we stood there in front of the building and I felt like crying she was so mean. She called me every filthy name she could think of. I guess I really hurt her leaving like I did. I don't suppose there is any way to change that now. You can't undo the past. Then I didn't see her anymore until she called one night and asked if she could see me. I agreed. And you can imagine how it turned out. Sex should never be like that. Then I didn't see her again for about a week. I needed to talk with someone that night and called her. She was alone and lonely too. So we ended up making the same mistake again. It got to be very sick. Afterward we both felt

bad. And I made up my mind not to see her again. Even if she
called in desperation. But it has been many weeks now and she
hasn't called. So I hope and trust she has found her way. She's
really a good person and deserves happiness. I think she'll do all
right too. And as I said I'm doing all right giving myself fully to
my work. I enjoy working with the people in my department and
my hours are pretty flexible. And already we are close to a circulation of a hundred thousand copies per month. It's a monthly
magazine. So much for myself and my world. It was really great
to hear that you are getting into things you find interesting. But
the Black Panther Party newspaper isn't the only Black publication around. Read *Stance*. Make sure you read it and let me know
what you think. After all it is for Black women. By the way I read
an article in the *Amsterdam News* about your Uncle Elmer Blake.
Doctor Blake. It said that he just won some sort of impressive
award for a book he wrote on the Harlem scene in the 1920s.
Should be an interesting book. I have always felt that the 1920s
would be a great time to have been alive and grown. Anyway this
letter is getting a bit long and I have work to do. Again I must say
it was good to hear from you. Keep in touch.
Yours, Al.

Dear Al: I have looked everywhere for *Stance* but apparently it is not for sale in Boston. No one seems to have heard of it here yet. Perhaps because it is a new publication. From what you say it sounds very interesting and I am anxious to see it. Please send me a copy. Guess what. In addition to all my other activities I have now taken up the guitar. I am studying with this really great guy from Berkeley who studied under world famous Andrés Segovia. And I really love the instrument. And it is good for my head to be making my own music. I love music so much. Did I tell you in my previous letter that I see my old friend Sara. Two weeks ago she had to give up her home and now lives in an apartment not far from here. She has gone through a lot but I think now she's growing stronger and opening to new areas of interest. She takes clay modeling on Wednesday nights with me. Her little girl Cynthia is growing so fast and she calls me Aunt Julie. Not that I encourage it. In fact it gives me a very strange feeling. One I can live without. One of these days when I meet Mister Right I want to have children. But I'm in no hurry. Did you ever read the autobiography of Malcolm X. It's a great great book if you haven't read it you should stop whatever you're doing right now and go out and buy a copy. By the way thanks for telling me about the article in the *Amsterdam News*. Mom bought a copy of Uncle Blake's book and I saw it last time I was at her place. You'd think he'd have sent us a copy but then I think he's always considered us stupid or something. The trouble with him is all his life he's been a stiff stuckup puritan. And my family tends to be free and open. Open to new ideas. Mom still asks about you. In fact I showed her your letter and she was happy about your success. She may write to you sometime. May even stop in to see you when she's in N. Y. I guess I told you about Dad losing his job. Now it appears he is planning to go to work for the NAACP. I have no direct contact with him. But he is in touch with Barbara. Mom and I hear about him through Barbara. He and Barbara were always close. He called Oscar once and talked with him for an hour. Oscar of course is with Mom. It just happened that Mom answered the phone when he called. And would you believe all Dad said to her was, May I speak to Oscar. Wouldn't even acknowledge her presence. Not even as much as a hello. Wow. He must be chang-

ing a lot because at least he was always respectful toward Mom.
But I'm not trying to understand it anymore. It is beyond me. Barbara is in Paris now and she hears from Dad a lot. She says the
French are cold people. Won't tolerate anyone who can't speak
French. Barbara of course speaks a little French. But I know what
she means because Paris turned me off too. White countries in
general turn me off. I love Africa. As you well know. I also en-
joyed teaching the history of Africa to black kids that time in
Brooklyn. May one day get back into this sort of work. It gives
me a very good feeling, working with children. You remember
my cousin, Gloria. In a letter from her I learn many things. Are
you ready for this. You remember The Corked Pussy Cat. Well
a Hollywood company has made a movie in which it is one of the
main scenes; but they're calling the place by another name. Gloria
says Rose Marie was recently pregnant. She may have gotten
pregnant last August up at Duck Pond. She really screws around
a lot. She's 16 years old now. Anyway they sent her to New York
for an abortion. But Rose Marie's relation to the family has been
altered by this whole experience. And my uncle being the type of
man he is compounds the situation. My cousin Patrick was drafted
last month but ran away to Canada and nobody has heard from
him since. I don't blame him. But it is sad that he may not be able
to come back home for many years. He was very close to his
mother, Aunt Alla. By the way Gloria says she's seeing a new
doctor who may really help her. I hope so. I recently ran into her
African friend. The one who was there at Duck Pond remember.
His name is Bill Gwala. He's a friend of a friend of mine, Clark
Nkosi. Who is also a friend of Odum. Remember Odum. Anyway
I have been dating Bill Gwala but not seriously. I think Africans
are mentally too far from me. There's always something there in
a relationship with an African that is not quite right for me. Any-
way he and I went out together several times. He asked about you.
Well I have to get ready for my modern dance class. And tonight
I'm going out dancing with Bill. Don't forget to send me a copy
of your magazine.
Peace, Julie.

Dear Julie: By now you should have the copy of *Stance* I sent. What do you think? This has been a hell of a week for me. I haven't stopped one minute. I must be going on nervous energy. I certainly have had little or no sleep. But I'm wrapped up in what I'm doing. The work is more and more exciting every day. I found your letter waiting yesterday when I returned from Fisk University in Tennessee where I spoke to the students there about *Stance*. I gave out a lot of free copies and I think we'll be getting many subscribers from that area as a result of my trip. It is in the area of paid circulation that I am trying to build *Stance*. Subscriptions mean more in my department than newsstand sales. Tomorrow I am to speak at New York University about *Stance*. I have been invited there by the Black students. They seem to have a great thing going, their own thing, and it's a good source to tap. I have always wanted to put my energy into something like this, something that takes me into contact with people. I am discovering that my life is turning out beautiful after all. Got to go now. Let me hear your reaction to *Stance*.
Yours, Al.

Dear Al: Here is my official response to *Stance*: I don't like it. What I dislike about it is its glossy smugness, its supercommercial jive hangups. The girl on the cover looks like she's squatting to take a youknowwhat. I mean the expression on her face is constipated. And the wig she's wearing looks like dimestore quality. And what happened to the color? She looks orange. And I've never seen any orange black people in my life. And why are there so many cigarette ads? I counted at least seven. Cigarette ads and makeup. The makeup I guess is all right, but I couldn't understand so many cigarette ads. Is it some sort of secret conspiracy to inflict all black women with cancer? You know genocide. I noticed your name is in 15th place on the list of staff personnel. I don't know why but somehow I expected you to be closer to the top. Another thing I found confusing was the fact that the table of contents did not always agree with the pages on which the various features and articles appeared. For example on page 26 there are these words: "The Plight of The Black Woman Novelist In Modern American Literature" by Ruth Smith, but according to the table of contents page 26 should contain: "Thirty-Five Views of Black Women on Black Men" by Nancy Giacchi. I looked through the entire publication at least seven times after reading everything in it and I couldn't find even a trace of the article by Nancy Giacchi. Was this a printer's error? Anyway, I did find the sections on beauty and food and home decoration interesting. The pictures of the grapes with the water drops on them was great. You should do more of this kind of stuff. I also liked the fantastic purple and green rug in the picture of a livingroom on page 61. I'd like to own one like that. The caption doesn't say where it can be bought. I was wondering if you could give me this information? No hurry because I don't have the bread at the moment. My allowance from Dad ended when he married Roslyn Carter. Anyway these are my responses to *Stance*. And I am sincerely sorry they were not more positive. And I hope you do not think badly of me for giving you my honest impression.
Until next time, Julie.

Dear Al: Having heard nothing from you in all these weeks I thought I'd write again, though I think you owe me a letter, since I was the one who wrote last, way back in November. Maybe it was the beginning of December. Anyway, here it is a new year. Barbara flew back from France to spend Christmas with us. It was great. We were all together at Mom's place. Dad didn't even call. Still, it was wonderful. I hope you had a pleasant holiday season. By the way, I saw another issue of *Stance* on a newsstand in Harvard Square. I looked through it and it certainly looked better than the first one. I thought you'd be pleased to hear this. The cover was great. Keep up the good work. I've been vaguely playing with the notion of going down to Mexico for awhile. You may remember I mentioned Clark Nkosi. We were friends for a long time and never thought of each other in romantic terms. That is until recently. Now he's been invited to teach in Mexico City and will be leaving here shortly. He wants me to go with him down there. I haven't made up my mind yet, but I will have to very soon. This is the first time I've started having an affair with a person who was at first a friend. It has always been the other way around. After an affair ends, the man and I become friends. Usually. As in our case. I often think of you, Al. But for a long time I couldn't bear to remember what happened between us. I was so hurt. I had expected us to be together for the rest of our lives. I think I resented you, too. As though our failure to make it was all your fault. I tend to be childish in this way, but I'm working on myself trying to do better. Anyway, with Clark things are different. We simply let things happen. I haven't made any elaborate plans to give the rest of my life to him. And I am sure the thought has never entered his mind. We both value our freedom. He's a brilliant man and he's writing a book. A novel about modern day Africa in which he's trying to show the interplay, exchange and conflict between the natives and the colonialists. I've read sections of it and it's great, sure to be a bestseller. Obviously, I have tremendous respect for him. But I won't go on about my affairs. It has been so long since I heard from you, I hardly know what to say. I hope your work is still going well. Write when you can.
Sincerely, Julie.

Dear Julie: I received your letters but was not able to answer before now because I have been both very busy and was in the hospital for a week. I spent a week in Harlem Hospital with two broken ribs and a broken jaw. I'm much better now. Back at work. It was kind of freakish the way it happened. I was in a bar near Times Square and got into a fight with a white guy. I don't remember what we were arguing about. They say we were arguing about something. But it turned out the place was filled with his friends and they all jumped me. I guess I'm lucky to be alive. I must have been very drunk because all I can remember is the bartender refusing to serve me a drink. But this must have been long before the fight started. Anyway, I'm still alive. My momma was my nurse. So I could not have had better care. For a week I stayed up there with Momma and Pop in their apartment after I was released from the hospital. It was good in a way because I got to know my pop a little better. He and I talked a lot while I was there. And he told me things about his childhood I never knew. The hard times he's had. And I think it gave me a greater respect for him as a person. Momma of course is Momma and she was simply great, both in the hospital and later. I can walk around now but not too fast. And I can talk, too, but not too fast. Sounds funny now but when it happened it wasn't so funny. And the crazy part is I've never gone out to pick a fight with anybody. But I've never let anybody fuck with me either. Ever since I was a little kid I've always drawn the line. Anyway, that's the big event in my recent history. I'm back at work now here and things have really piled up. I have a helper, too. A young guy fresh out of college. I'm training him. Teaching him the business. So he'll know everything about circulation I know. Anyway, take care and if you go to Mexico watch out, you might get a suntan.
Sincerely yours, Allen Morris.

Dear Allen Morris: I've been busy writing letters, letters, letters. And receiving them. It seems all at once everybody I've ever known has written to me. Anki and Christer are back in Stockholm. They say it is very dark and cold there. As usual. But they spend part of the year there every year. My friend Nicholas Zieff has just surprised us all by getting married. He has married a lovely woman. I think she's simply delightful. She is also a teacher and they have a lot more in common. The wedding was small since this was the second time for them both. A few days ago I ran into José Cruz and he asked if he could stop by sometime. Tonight we're having supper together in an Indian restaurant. He's just been promoted on his job and is in good spirits. He's a wonderful person and I've always admired him. My old friend Johnny Hawkins was recently in town for an engagement at a nightclub. Saw the notice in a local paper but didn't go to see him. Though I was tempted to. Despite the hassles, Johnny and I had good times together. And looking back on the relationship I realize I loved him deeply and probably still do. And always will. Sorry I must end this letter so quickly, but I have tons of letters to write.

Sincere regards, Julie Ingram.

Dear Julie My Friend: Thank you for your recent letter. This is just a note to acknowledge having received it. I am head over heels in work. Still training my helper who is turning out to be a very good worker. Take care.
Sincerely yours, Al.

Al: Please forgive my haste. Am seriously thinking of moving to Mexico City. Making plans. But haven't been feeling well lately. A friend of mine, an African named Hourari, was shot two days ago at an airport in Ghana. I don't know details. Trying to find out exactly what happened. Though it may not be possible. This leaves me deeply distressed. What kind of world are we living in?
Best regards, your friend, Julie.

My Dearest Julie: Do you remember the blind colored man I helped across the street that time in Boston? Well, I've been thinking about him a lot. How he took me to be a white person. This self-hatred in our race. How we kill each other. It is a painful situation. We here at *Stance* are having a famous Negro psychologist write an article on the subject for one of our spring issues. Hope you are well.

Your friend, Al.

Dear Al: Clark Nkosi left for Mexico three days ago. I finally decided not to go with him. Mom needs me and besides all my best friends are here. I am planning to step up my activity. I am a very active physical person. In addition to modern dance and clay modeling, I am planning now to start classes in filmmaking, pottery and poetry, acrobatics and puppetry, drama and jewelry making. I had also thought about figure drawing but I probably won't have time for so much. I am also looking for a job, one that will allow me time to do other things.

Dear Julie Ingram: I received your recent letter and am happy to know that you are still happy and well. Am working hard and am also very happy. Keep in touch.
Sincerely yours, Allen Morris.

Virginia

L ATE IN APRIL VIRGINIA and I decided to live together and on
May 2nd we had her stuff moved into my Perry Street apartment. We were crowded as hell but it felt good not having to separate at night.

One day we were walking on 8th Street and I saw a necklace
of red beads in a jewelry store window. I bought them for her and
she put them on immediately.

Right now it is sticky and hot though it's fall. Yesterday I
listened to a publisher on the radio. The interviewer had a crisp
voice. He says he's annoyed by the industry. The publisher as-
sures him that it helps people understand each other. Virginia
works in publishing.

I had trouble finding a parking space at eleven in the morning.
The car is a pain in the ass. The city is worse.

Virginia's mother stopped by. She says Virginia's husband just
died. I like Virginia's mother, though she does not speak to me.
Virginia's mother sat politely on the edge of the couch while
telling us the news. Virginia blew her nose into a Kleenex tissue.
Virginia's mother paused and sniffed.

The epidemic strikes again. I'm not going out till it passes.

While lying in bed naked beside Virginia the phone rings. It's Virginia's mother again. While they talk I stroke Virginia's vagina. It's Saturday in the summer.

There was nothing wrong with me but for some reason I lost confidence in my health. I went to a private doctor and to several clinics. They all told me there was nothing wrong. "You're in excellent health. There's nothing wrong," said one doctor, with a toothy smile.

I had a pain in my shoulder.

I had a pain in my neck.

I had a pain in my back.

I had a pain in my stomach.

I had a pain in my head.

I had a pain in my sleep.

After awhile I began to live a little more easily with the threat of the madman. Virginia and I bought a large plant. It brought some new cheer to me.

In time, and for reasons equally unknown, the confidence in my health returned and I stopped wasting my money on doctors. Virginia was pleased.

I concerned myself with routine matters: I studied the causes of unnatural bleeding. Answered letters. Gave the dog a bath. Went to the Bronx Zoo. Searched for a lover.

Lately I do most of the cooking since I am a house husband. Virginia and I are eating mostly vegetables: green peas mushroom red cabbage acorn squash beans sweet potatoes carrots eggplant bean sprouts and lots of wheat bread with crab meat. Virginia dislikes steak and chicken. She reads a lot of poetry.

Virginia wears the coil. One of the side effects is unnatural bleeding. Virginia's mother says double parking isn't allowed on her street.

Across the street they're demolishing a building to build a new apartment building of two and three bedroom units. We buy Deep Park Spring Water but it doesn't help the noise.

Many people are already moving to Connecticut.

When Virginia got pregnant we took the thing out of her and demolished it. Virginia doesn't believe we are killers. She says, "It was already dead. Let's go on a protein diet."

This morning it is raining, just a drizzle. For months we have lived with the noise and dirt. Virginia has decided to take dancing lessons. I exercise every morning. Who needs to dance.

They've decided to level the whole block of old buildings. Now the plan is to build a complex. Virginia is complex, too: she now drinks and cries a lot. I eat eggs and feel helpless.

Painters have invaded our apartment. They are sloppy and un-friendly. We now live at the edges of their life there.

The rain has stopped.

Virginia's husband is in the ground in the Bronx. Virginia stopped wearing the red beads.

Virginia has a vacation coming. I always have trouble finding a parking place for the car. Most of the streets are off limits from 8 AM to 6 PM every day except Saturday and Sunday. We have decided not to take it on vacation with us. I have a new pain.

The plan now is to get tickets. The painters have gone and life has returned to "normal." It's Monday in the winter. Next door the karate lessons are in full force.

The man parked behind my car hits its rear trying to get out. He said he was sorry and I got out and looked at the damage. There was little but the man wanted to fight anyway. He pulled alongside me and said, "What's the matter you don't like my I'm sorry?" I looked directly into his eyes and realized that, like all our neighbors, he was absolutely insane. I had a pain in my neck so I said nothing. He drove away mumbling to himself.

In the mail this morning: a letter from Scotland. I don't know anybody in Scotland. At seven this morning the trip hammers started.

I should go to Scotland.

I should go to Connecticut.

I should go to Virginia. But in Virginia I'm not necessarily safe. Isn't there a lot of noise in Virginia too?

The Vase and the Rose

T HE VASE WITH NOTHING in it. Think about that. There was a girl I used to go with. She could come in five minutes. I married her and she could not. Think of a flight of dark stairs. Like lungs, a bird trapped in there, trying to get out. I think you understand.

She says, "Hold me within your goodness. See we eat together sleep together, together we each go out into our own separate moments alone, alone yet sometimes minus your presence only your voice on the phone. . . . It's very difficult to explain. There is a connection. When we touch."

This is life at home.

He says to her, "Discover me falling through wet weeds under the brick moon. My orange coffee table floating in the rum sky of your life. I am unaltered from infection to insulin. Discover me tumbling down your sleep with bricks in my fists."

I watch them talk to each other.

I listen to them.

"I listen to the crickets and watch your eyes."

His reponse: "Vapid and unaltered night clouds continue to drown us and our future and furniture as we discover and rediscover ourselves."

She, Sara, in black slip, lifts beads to her neck. The yorkie sleeps on the round rug near her. Sara is standing before the mirror. He, Sam, has gone out. The vase is sad in its corner.

Sara is trying to remember Sam's dream about bricks in his fists. The room is lined with rows of books.

Was he falling or ascending.

Each shape repeats itself. She likes the view of her pink body. Yet she wants to smash the mirror. Feelings, for Sara, are never simple. She is the best friend of my wife who cannot have an orgasm. They are members of a group of women that get together to compare their feelings and thoughts, especially about relations with men.

She dresses, wanting Sam to understand how to hold her within his goodness, whatever that means. In an orange sack dress, wearing glasses that mean the eyes are helpless things, she skips out like a child. She's bright and light. The ends of her fingers touch. She is, for this moment, in touch with herself.

She returns and makes tea on the orange coffee table. Sam is due any minute. She changes the record on the record player.

Sam arrives. They change positions in relation to each other.

They are in the basement now.

Now on the roof.

Out front waving down a taxi.

"I should send you home to your mother," Sam says, "you're too young, you change too quickly; you're going to break my heart!" He throws his right fist into the palm of his left hand. "Damnit! I can't stand it!"

The vase is still empty. I'm thinking what I might do about this. I remain still. I am in motion. When she breaks she allows me to enter. I am passive-aggressive. My reasons are willful. I am moving from this place in their lives. I will not take Sara, I will not take Sam, with me. My spirit is in me. Sadness and joy are in them through me. I ache yet I am happy. I'm trapped yet I am free. I shall survive, they will not.

The three of us are deeply ignorant yet we keep trying to reach each other. The long arm of his body reaches out to touch her body. This body overcomes its accidents. It retreats for safety, fumbles in the darkness. It feeds itself. It sleeps and it hums. It is a lonely body as it moves silently through its days. It grows soft and it comes. It leaves hot spaces in bed. Her body leaves cool impressions. Sam's body is heavy and, at times, dull, sluggish. Trees survive all three bodies. These bodies close around each other desperately trying to stay warm. We hope that there is a place for power in the body. We dream of the darkness of the lungs within the bodies. What is trapped in those lungs?

Sam complains: "I went out and down for you, Sara, so long, godamnit, it is about time you go down to the river and search the boats for me. Bring up the boats to the shore. Since we are both visitors, bring me a visitor. Sleep with me and love me, hold me. I can't sleep. I am so passionate I can die of it. I went way out and I cannot sleep well."

This confession brings tears to her eyes. This is merely an example of their uneasy home life. I am tired of watching them talk to each other like this.

At other times Sam tries to pour that passion into words: "Do not explain your body to me, Sara. I am a sailor going deeper into the land, exploring, seeking wells. I rediscover all the seas! Down there, my arms my legs my spine, all of me, my body, floats, till it reaches yours, with that cocksure smile you sometimes give me. What a joke you say. I take off your starched uniform and dry your hair. I cover you with my body. We make love in the open."

Sara is modeling for an art class. She sits there, a girlish body. Her legs crossed and her arms supporting her lean body. Bobbed hair and swimming trunks. She is pink and lean.

"The sunlight in here," says Sam, "is just what I need this morning."

Sara: "We live here now, honey, in this dim room where I lie down in a blazing streak of sunlight—like this—every morning, facing east. This is the only place to read. I stopped going out. Even modeling is a bore. There is nothing out there but the city. Old people sitting on park benches feeding peanuts to birds. Maybe a cute boy, a pretty girl. An old woman walking a small dog. . . . "

There is an emptiness in Sara's voice that Sam has not heard lately.

He tries to comfort her. "Finally when your interesting argyle-plaid dress is off you seem neutralized and I can see the green of your long eyelids turn blue. I like drawing circles with your eye-shadow stick on your stomach. I hang my tweed jacket in your dark closet. You realize what I am about to do. Do you?"

They were soon making love while high and could not control the steam of it during summer nights. They turned and turned in the huge damp bed, caught in the twisted sheets. Make this out: Sam pulls Sara's legs and arms apart and bites deeply into her neck. She screams, birds flying out of her mouth, with joy. Then they both snapped—opened into the whole universe—coming together.

Then Sam went down into her mines and did six months for her because he loved her so madly.

By midafternoon Sara placed one red rose in the vase and though no sunlight reached it, the rose did wonders for the room.

Fun and Games

MARY JONES AND LOLA MARIE JONES are not related. In fact, Lola is white, Mary black. Mary actually looks white and Lola is a dark complexioned white woman. Jeannie Devore is another story. She left two months ago.

I always tried to avoid roommates. I like plants better yet I somehow get stuck with roommates. Right now Mary is my roommate. When other women call me, Mary waters the plants.

Mary likes to make love.

Jeannie did not.

Lola likes to make love though she does not know much about it. Some day somebody will teach her.

I met Lola at an African dance concert. She was sharing an apartment with a nurse. I slept there a lot before meeting Mary. Then Lola found a man she liked better than me. But we continued to see each other anyway.

Lola told me one night she and her new lover went for a walk across the Brooklyn Bridge. Half way across she got down on her knees and gave him the blowjob of his life. She said it gave her strange thrills. While she told me this story we were making love.

Lola used to joke about marrying. She'd say, "Let's get married, move to a farm, and start breeding. I want to cook eggs and bacon in the mornings for you and a house full of brats." Then we'd laugh about her imaginative story.

Lola finally left New York. It was too much for her.

Jeannie called one day from California and I said, "Who?" and
she said, "Jeannie," and I said, "You've got the wrong number."
Then she wrote and said, "I tried to call you but I kept getting the
wrong number."

Mary told me: "You are just the man for me: young, dark and
handsome, sensitive, intelligent. When you finish school and are
firmly set in your profession, then what."
   "We'll move into a larger place."
We found a larger place overlooking the Hudson. We felt like
rich folks. Mary told me about her previous boy friend: he struck
her in the face once. He was a graduate law student. She moved
out and promised herself she'd never take up with a white boy
again.

Mary goes to work in midtown. I have no idea what she does.
I keep trying to get the super to remove this old dusty wall to wall
carpet. I'm sure it's been here since the turn of the century.

Mary is having a miscarriage. I ask if there's anything I can do.
She says no just stay out of my way.

We bought plants and filled the living room windows with
them. Mary bought guppies and filled the tank she's had since high
school.
   A letter from Lola asks me to return the pictures of herself that
she gave me.
   I send them. She's now in Wisconsin. Why Wisconsin.

"I'm bringing to this relationship a lot of problems."
"So that's the nature of things."
"This is my space over here, that's your's over there. That way
we don't get confused."

Mary's parents wanted to meet me. They liked me and I liked
them. It was all very cozy. The four of us went on a cruise up the
Hudson and spent one whole Sunday at Bear Lake with the Puerto
Ricans. I like Puerto Rican music.

"There was a boy I loved when I was twelve. His name was Dud Novak! We used to smooch a lot. I thought we would grow up and marry."

"There was a girl I loved desperately when I was a kid. I never said a word to her. I don't think she ever knew I loved her so completely."

Mary wants to know about Jeannie and Lola. I tell her all about Jeannie and Lola. I also want to tell her about Sue and Ruth and Betty and Marie but she's not interested. She wants to know about Jeannie and Lola.

Jeannie was very pale with red hair and she read books real fast. She was smart and trippy.

Lola was clumsy. Poor Lola.

I have a snapshot of Betty. Betty is dark and beautiful. She married a doctor. They are now divorced.

"What are we going to do with our lives?"

"I sorta thought we were doing something already."

"You know what I mean. Where are we going?"

We go to the annual West Indian Day Parade in Harlem. It's a drag: a wet ugly day and the steppers are sluggish and the floats skimpy.

We walk two blocks to visit Mary's grandmother. I like Mary's grandmother because she likes me. We always hug and kiss. She came to New York sixty years ago on a boat.

Carmen called me. I had forgotten about her. She had to remind me. "Oh, Carmen, how are you?"

Carmen told me she was unhappily married to a dentist and she wanted to know if we could meet secretly somewhere. I was bored with Mary so I said yes.

I met Carmen. She had changed. Her hair was now blond. I liked her better the other way.

We had lunch together, then in her Mustang drove to a motel

in Brooklyn where we made love all afternoon. It was fun but she's getting fat.

Mary is watering the plants again.

Carmen never touched liquor. Mary never smoked cigarettes. I'm watching television for a change: a green chicken jumps over a red mountain range. An old man with a white beard puffs on a corncob pipe. He takes off his sailor cap and holds it toward a passing lady. Another man smoking a cigarette is on horseback riding through a valley. Mother Nature suddenly appears. I drift back to Carmen, comparing her to Mary. It's unfair. But so what.

Little Alfred is Mary's brother. He comes to see us. He is short and fat like his father. His clothes are supermod. He wears white silk shirts with large floppy sleeves. He sports a huge awesome afro and wears platforms.

Sometimes he brings his girl friend, Malissa, with him. She's a colored redhead with green eyes. They are both heavily into dope.

Little Alfred tells me his problems. He says the only life for a black dude is the Life. By this he means ripping off people, anybody. He is an interesting young man because he never wears gabardine slacks. His girl friend likes television. She can sip bourbon very slowly. This is something Little Alfred has not learned to do.

I kiss Mary. She waters the plants.

Lola called to tell me she'd moved back to New York and was just wondering how I was doing. She knows about Mary. I said, "I'm all right, how about you."

"I have to talk with you," she said in a strained voice. "It's very urgent."

We met nearby at a restaurant on Broadway. She seemed taller. "I met this man named Mel and I changed my name to Juanita. I think I want to marry him. But there's one problem: He likes the bottom best, always wants to do it on his back. I don't know if I can live with that. And his lips are thin. Maybe I can't live with thin lips and being on top."

I kissed her and took off her huge blue sunglasses then kissed each of her eyelids.

"What'd you think?"

I told her to take it easy.

Juanita and I are making love in her hotel room in Chelsea. She's improved. I'm tempted to marry her to save her from Mel. But too many other aspects are wrong: she's still too tall and not bright enough. She still wants brats and she can't read a book as fast as Jeannie Devore. Where is Jeannie Devore anyway?

Jeannie Devore is walking along 8th Street when I come out of the Art Theatre after watching that sad movie, *Last Tango in Paris*. We throw our arms around each other and kiss passionately then look at each other. Her eyes are still sharp and fast.

We go for coffee but do not talk about the past. She talks about California. I tell her about Mary. Then she tells me, "I've changed my name: it's Mildred Maraventano. I met this woman and we fell in love with each other. Her name was Jeannie and since we did not both want to be Jeannie at the same time I had to find another name. And Mildred Maraventano was always my favorite name."

I asked her if she was still with Jeannie.

"Yes, we live together in the Village but I haven't given up men. I think about you a lot."

Mary waters the plants again while telling me about Zelda Fitzgerald and what a rotten bastard Scott was. I'm wondering if Mary has ever read *Hansel and Gretel*.

Mary comes in from work. She says, "Sit down, Jerry, I have something to tell you."

I followed her instructions. Surely something was up. I watched her eye twitch. The contact was probably bothering her again.

"What's up?"

"I'm in love with a man who makes a checklist and I'm going

to leave you for him. He listens to me when I talk to him. He's
not impatient with catalogs either. We work together."

I laughed nervously. "Well . . . "

"I know, there's nothing to say."

"I guess not. You got it all figured out. Did you do any research
on this thing before making such a big decision?"

"You made the decision for me."

"How?"

"By snoring at night, by not liking eggplant. It's pointless, too
much to go into."

I am now watering the plants.

Number Four

THIS IS ONE OF THE last days. She is upstairs. I can hear her typing letters, searching for answers. I am down here, packing, ready to move again; surveying the things that have gathered around my life, my body. I hate them; they weigh too much. She is polite but not friendly. Yet we do not hate the final days. I spend most of my time out, in another world, touching it, other women, knowing it. That world responds. A year from now I will pack again. Start all over. Before I leave I say to her, "I will wash your sink full of dirty dishes." She likes the idea so I don't do it.

We are packing and we are angry.

Now that the end is here it is proper to look back to the beginning, to the middle, to the recent past. Without meaning I cannot go on.

He says he can't go on.

In the beginning she wore a raspberry ribbon on her head. On her feet she wore shoes with a mouth at the toe.

She is dry and intense and fat. At other times she is slender and pretty.

She was busted for possession of too much food, too much hope and dope, too much wisdom and knowledge. This is where I come into the picture. In prison she is writing poems. Sends me one, falls in love with me. According to prison regulations she can write to only four persons.

Do I want to be number four?

Does he want to be in the picture at all?

"What can a drug-ridden virgin look forward to at twenty-three?" She wants to know. "Coma constipation and brain damage." Next time she will stay away.

Her letters arrive on raspberry stationery. My words in response arrive at the tip of my tongue but go nowhere near her ear.

Out now, she dyes her hair orange and changes her name to Raspberry. Previously it was Straw. I sleep with her. The bed squeaks. Our separate thoughts expand in the room. "Listen," she says, "I want you. A sadness chokes you. All my life it has been this way." She wants to be in the picture.

Beer and cake on the table. She drinks liquor and wears a tan velvet hat. Call her Sweetpie Straw. Her thoughts are all afterthoughts. She eats raspberries and cream from a green bowl.

She gets drunk and does the nasty in public. Steps between spaces left by tables in juke joints singing dirty songs, rolling her belly.

What can a woman of twenty-four with a prison record expect? Impotence hangover anxiety withdrawal delusions anxiety insomnia. What happened to the raspberry ribbon?

The bed squeaks. Think about it. Think about the blunt, broken way she and I touch each other.

She has her legs crossed and there is a cigarette dangling from her mouth, to the left, its tip glowing. She is a Hollywood ghost against the darkness of my sleep. She's slightly above my bed, looking down at me. "Who are you?"

"One day I will leave you."

Her permissive black eyes shine from her blue complexion. She has no discipline.

I am in the hospital and the doctor comes in to tell me that a strange woman is here to see me. He says she is highly respected and I say do I know her.

He brings her in and she's wearing the ribbon.

She's pink and I'm brown. A very white girl she walks across the street, throwing her hips from side to side. She is not wearing a ribbon.

For six months — while I was away — she did not know she was a woman holding a child — an imaginary child. A dark blue mass of flesh, she had no meaning. Lumps in her belly, in her face. The child's head was out of focus, hanging slightly forward. Asleep.

Long ago, deep in her, there was a dream of a cowboy walking blindly on the desert under the bright sun. He was half crazy hungry lost thirsty. A stretch of purple, perhaps sky or land, slid into her life, like some sort of liquid moving under glass. She was in the prison of herself, then one morning, for no reason she could name, her water broke and she and her baby were born, like this, holding each other, and just moving back and forth, in a rocking motion, gently, back and forth. Orange hair, a rich blue undergarment hanging loosely down her side, and the rest of the child, eggshell white, with her long pink fingers supporting its chin.

I see her sitting in a flat white room. She is not withdrawn. Her hair is no longer orange.

She watches me as I scratch my way through a screen of fishhooks. The obstacle will be barbed wire. This is the stuff of our relation to each other.

She's dyed her hair red and she's now wearing red clothes. This woman, a question. Her face is framed. She's back in school but not learning anything. She stirs in milk. Shakes well. She chops carrots and types. Washes her slips and stockings. Pours and scrapes batter. She uses a wide cooking pan. Washes her hair. Soaks in the tub. She continues beating her eggs. Her eyes are no longer permissive.

She does not write love letters on raspberry paper.

I am watching him.

He stoops to avoid the limbs of dangling trees. The only light in his life comes from the light in her eyes. The sky opens there in those two places. Rob is his name. Rob is my name. Nora is her name. Raspberry Nora. Ashamed of her prison record especially now that she is respectable: a teacher in a school. Real class. Here, in our place, a simple mirror. A window opens on a yard of red leaves. "Hold me." He enters her. She captures him. "Hold me. Hold me closer!" The only darkness inside his life is in Nora. He is especially aware of it while she's washing her slips.

They go for a walk in the woods. Bluejays, cigarette butts, campfire ashes, stunted trees. A lake, a lakeside.

She slips away to be with her woman lover. They touch the nipples of their breasts together. Silk openings. Something closer, closes. In the darkness, many imaginary men, many women, quietly move. Is this a secret orgy? Touching, dreaming. Muscles snap. Hair. Skin. Fingers circle other fingers. I wonder why I am left out of the huge struggle of unnatural breathing. But isn't it natural? "Open your arms." "Ouch!"

When the lights are turned on they each retreat into themselves, politely smiling or smirking. This is close to the last day.

Is this amnesia? The landscape is alive with mice. I'm searching for her but she's apparently not around. Has she been arrested again?

Why have I resigned myself to lying here facing my hands? We live here in our lives. Shadows. Corners. Green shades with light coming through. We are not happy, we are unhappy. In the kitchen there is a white sink. A purple broom. Outside people are still moving along.

She is upstairs now trying to plan her future. Her typewriter stops. The phone rings. I can hear her talking but I can't make out what she's saying. Probably talking with her lover. Her lover works in the school where she works.

Apparently I did become number four without fully wanting that role. Now it is ending.

It will take two years to recover.

IV

Maggy: A Woman of the King

MAGGY IS RUNNING TOWARD us with a broken halo held high. Yes yes, it's a halo! It's glowing in the sun. Her face is crabby, red and dirty. "The cops!" she cries.

Her dry wooden leg causes her to creak. It gives her an awkward rhythm.

"I just got back from the welfare building!" she says, "and the cops followed me all the way." Panting she continues: "I think they plan to raid my apartment! Quick, help me hide the stuff!"

The stuff she wants to hide is all the new stuff she bought with the stolen money. Also she probably wants to hide the dope. Her old leather-like skin is wet.

We're standing on the corner watching her. We're calm. We ain't guilty of nothing. I'm not the leader but I say, "Sure, Maggy, we'll help. Hey guys!"

The cops found nothing and an hour later Maggy, in her baggy dress, comes down. "Say, I think they're planning a raid on the Queen." The Queen is the hotel down the block. My best friend is the desk clerk. His name is. Oh, I better not tell you. It might get him in trouble.

The fellas look at Maggy with despair and dismay. They don't want to be bothered but my friend—call him Joe—might be in for trouble.

"Hey guys! Let's check it out!"

The four of us trotted away from the entranceway of the King in the direction of the Queen.

We knew Joe was a heavy dealer and pimp and could easily get busted.

Maggy yelling: "Each minute you lose could be extremely unfortunate for Joe! Make haste!"

But it was a wild goose chase. Joe was fine. No cops in sight.

I'm having a conference with Maggy. It's two days later. She's sitting on the Coke crate by the Coke machine. I'm on the bottom step. She's smoking a Camel.

"Little Daddy," she says, "I broke my halo."

"You what?"

" Running yesterday I dropped it and broke it. Yesterday was a bad day all day. In the welfare office somebody put out a cigarette on my leg."

"The good one?"

"What'd you mean the good one both are good. My wood is as good as my flesh. You some kind of moralist?"

"Sorry, Maggy." I stood up and got a Coke from the machine. "I thought you were rich now why do you still need welfare?"

"Rich my ass! I spent that five hundred in two days. Sometimes I think poor folk ain't got no business with money. They don't know what to do with it. I myself is a good example."

"I saw all those boxes you came in with."

"Yeah. Hats."

"You mean you bought *hats*?"

"Mostly hats and a few caps."

"But Maggy, *why*?"

"To keep my *head* covered. How do you like this one?"

It seemed strange, a green wool 1920s style floppy hat with a red band and a feather cattily jutting from the side stuck down in the band. "Nice," I said.

I'm in Maggy's room with her. She's showing me the broken halo. "It won't stay up by itself anymore."

I'm laughing now. "I've heard that one before!" I carefully examine the halo then hand it back to her.

"Maybe if Joe sets up a really big job for me, say, a place like the Chase Manhattan Bank, I could make a killing then buy a new halo. This one is thirty one years old. It was on its last leg. Just think! A brand new halo!" She suddenly looks sad. "But they're so expensive! A good one costs between ten and twenty thousand."

"Well," I said with a smirk, "in the meantime you have the hats."

The cops came into the lobby and asked Smitty, the desk clerk, for Maggy's room number. Smitty is a chickenshit dude. He could have told them Maggy had moved but he started shaking. Said: "I don't think she's here but her room is right up there at the top of the stairway. The first door!"

Naturally they went up and knocked and Maggy — not suspecting trouble — opened the door.

They took her away. I was leaning against the Coke machine smoking a Camel as they escorted her out. She was wearing a yellow hat with a blue bird attached to its side.

As she passed she glanced at me and winked.

After they were clearly out of the building I went over to the desk and grabbed Smitty by the front of his shirt. I didn't say anything. I just shook him and with my other hand slapped his face about five times. He started crying and shaking.

When I released him he folded up on the floor behind the desk. I didn't want to finish my Coke so I poured the remainder of it on his head.

Party with Masks

I T'S A PARTY—I don't know how I got here, but it's a party all right. It's raining—apparently I came through the rain. Strange since I've recently sworn not to get wet. It's so improbable that I'm really here. . . . Everything is hazy. But I'm sure I'm in Harlem. I must have been drunk now for . . . I don't know how many days, though I thought I'd stopped drinking.

Anyhow we're in the school building and they've turned off the lights. Candles are burning and everybody's dressed in strange costumes. Funny. People are clowning and dancing in crêpe paper. So far I haven't recognized anybody I know.

Now I recognize Mrs. Null who has not bothered to camouflage herself. She's sitting on the dimly lit stage, front and center. I go directly up. "Hi, how are you!" I'm overjoyed to recognize somebody but she doesn't remember me. The curse of old age or meeting or knowing too many people! She murmurs a stingy greeting.

At this moment the entire party is thrown into a frenzy by so much quick, frantic action coming from the far end of the auditorium, that my hurt-feelings are quickly suppressed. I jump off the stage and push my way through the crowd, trying to see what is happening.

A friend of mine, Walker, is shouting at somebody: "You dirty, dirty *bastard!*"

The people surrounding him, decked out as dogs, cats, rats, sheep, bats, goats, silk-worms, rabbits, lions, werewolves and snakes, are reacting verbally: "*Ohhhhhh!*" and: "How horrible!" and "My God!" and: "He's killing that poor silk-worm, he's stomping that poor silk-worm!"

Somebody knocks against me. I can see over the shoulder of a mule after I move its ear back: Walker is kicking the silk-worm. Walker — or at least his voice, is coming from this huge, fat sheep, shaggy as a grizzly. The silk-worm is on the floor whimpering and shrieking.

I'm still trying to figure out who the worm is when I realize I want out. I can't stand this sort of confusion! I try to move toward the door but it's difficult to get between the people. In the process I see Anna. She's dressed as Tanith, the fertility goddess of Phoenician Carthage. She's looking for Kronos she says. We embrace each other — it's impossible to say anything and be heard.

I look out the window: it's still raining.

I reach the doors leading to the lobby and go through, feeling the cleanness of escape, the way you feel when you first start talking to someone in his own language while still thinking in your own. In other words you don't *completely* escape.

I go down to the boys toilet in the basement but I can't get in because it's so jammed with weird creatures. Though my bladder is in trouble I refuse to piss in a corner. Or maybe I will piss in a corner.

At this point I remember the swimming pool. Hope the room isn't locked. On the way to the pool I realize that Anna is following me! I feel her breathing on my neck. She must be high on grass!

"Where you going, Straight?"

She calls me Straight because I don't smoke grass.

The door is locked. I get down and peep through the hole. Inside a whole bunch of strange animals are jumping around in the water. A werewolf is standing on the diving board ready to jump.

"What'd you see?" asks Tanith.

"Cow jumping over the moon."

"Funny."

I'm still looking through the hole. I see Narcissus chasing somebody dressed as a monkey. Around and around the pool.

Rocking playfully up and down on the diving board is a werewolf looking very evil.

"What'd you see?" Tanith is standing close.

"Here, look!"

She does. "Who are those people?"

"How should I know?"

Meanwhile someone walking like an old person, small of bone, comes into the passageway where we're standing before the locked door, and the voice, "Oh, there you are, dearie, I've been looking *every*where for you!" The figure gets closer and it's obviously one of the Furies, a goddess of guilt. I'm now sure it's Mrs. Null's voice. "Anna," she says to Tanith, "would you please scratch my back for me, dearie? This blasted old crepe paper is itching something awful, and *heavens*! it's so hot! There're so *many* people here! I never would have come if I had known it would be like *this*!" She looks at me, touches my arm. "Clay is such a nice, intelligent young man, and I respect him, but he should have known better than to invite me to something like this!" (I suspect that she doesn't know that *I'm* standing next to her. You know how old folks are.)

I don't remember inviting her but then I was drunk for days, right. Now Tanith is scratching the old woman's back. And saying, "By the way, did you come all the way down here to find *me* to scratch your back?"

"Huh?" Mrs. Null pretends she can't hear when she has no immediate answer. "Huh?"

Tanith repeats her comment.

Mrs. Null ignores her completely this time. "Over, dearie, just a little bit over to the left."

I start laughing. Hysterically. Falling against the wall. As Mrs. Null shuffles away she is talking to herself: "Stupid niggers, stupid niggers . . . "

Desperately I take out my godhead and pee against the wall, golden sparks. . . . Tanith is pretending not to see me. She turns away.

"What's this door here lead to?" Tanith is shaking the knob of a door directly across from the poolroom door.

"It's probably a broom closet or something." She opens the door which *does* conceal a broom closet. The super has a note tacked inside on the far wall: "This is a warning! Do Not Remove Anything From This Closet! Violators Are Subject To Serious Punishment. B. H. Johnson." Tanith turns to me. "Shit! Bring your fine ass on in here!" And she takes my hand.

We're inside now in total darkness. I feel her hot breath on my face. My back is against the wall. She's leaning against me.

Outside someone is banging on the pool door.

She begins to fumble with me, my belly under my shirt. She kisses my neck. She groans. "I'm thirty-five and very horny!"

At this point the door opens and Mrs. Null says, "Anna, dearie, are you in there?"

A streak of light has flooded us.

Tanith doesn't answer—she groans.

The door closes and for a moment I think Mrs. Null has left us alone until I hear her breathing. She's in here with us.

Mrs. Null clears her throat. "Anna," she says, "I can hear you breathing. You're there, aren't you?"

"No."

"I knew you were there."

Anna's hand has found its way down into my pants.

Suddenly lightning strikes in the sky outside. Where else would the lightning strike?

"Anna," says Mrs. Null, "Walker is looking for you. He's wandering around upstairs trying to find you. Why don't you run along and let him know you're all right? I'll take good care of the closet till you get back."

"Walker? I don't want to see Walker!"

I feel Mrs. Null's hands gripping my face. She kisses my cheek. I cringe—thankful for the darkness.

I realize—with renewed impact—that I want *out*! With energy and motivation springing from a primal level, I burst out of the closet leaving the two women there.

I run madly along the passageway, up the steps, down the hallway, and pushing open the swing door, out into the cold night air, running down the steps—skipping every two steps.

Old

I N THE MORNING THESE DAYS simple pleasure for you is sunlight. You can count on it. In the shade you are nervous.

You close your heavy eyelids and you are gripped by an uneasy peace. Small pains do not really count. Pain suspended on the limbs of drugs is a way of having someone in the room with you when it is four in the morning and you can't sleep. And in the morning the sun will come, again.

You close your eyes knowing that the reality of this moment cannot be moved to another location. The woman next to you smells. But such things you can live with. You live inside a musty place anyway. After all, she cleans and feeds you, she cares for you. Who else would care for you. For over thirty years now while the community was turning black. You haven't been out in ten years, legs too weak, arms too weak. You're old but surely you don't feel that way. How does old feel?

The woman in the room with you right now is sewing and rocking herself in your rocker. She too has lived here in this building in this black neighborhood for over thirty years. She's the office manager, she rents apartments when people move out. She makes sure dogs are not brought into the building, she makes sure families moving in do not have children and when the elevator isn't working she calls the elevator man.

You clear your throat and open your eyes.

The woman is talking to you.

"He died in the war."

You wonder, who died in which war. This is part of a conversation you have taken part in for a long time and many times in this room. Most of your life has been spent in this room or in other rooms listening to this conversation or another.

Her thin lips disappear inside her mouth. You wonder why all her dresses are so snug around the neck.

You pretend to listen to the war story but you are really remaking your own childhood again. You borrow playmates from the street below, those you saw today and yesterday. You play tricks on them. Steal their toys and run. They throw rocks at you. Try to dress like you. You can't hide, everywhere you hid they find you. They keep asking you questions about the war. Which war?

You are asleep and the woman is watching you. She seems to view you with sadness and tenderness. You are a fat old man with a heavy red face. Your fingers are swollen and your nails are short.

When the question of death comes up the woman pretends she can't hear. She says, "Huh? Did you say something?"

One day you look at her. "Who's the young colored woman in the apartment next to mine?"

"Oh, you've seen her, huh?"

"Yes, on the back porch this morning. Emptying her garbage. I was out for the sun. Beautiful girl."

You try to remember the garbage going down the chute. You see instead yourself going down the drain. You enter the ocean. The ocean enters the universe.

The woman rents a room to a young community organizer and soon he's dating the colored woman.

You're wheeling yourself down the hall one day when you meet him and you ask, "What do you do?"

"We do a lot of knocking on doors trying to get people interested in helping themselves. Everybody is asleep in the world. We simply try to wake them."

"Doors, huh?"

"Lots of doors."

You know he's taken the small room and you imagine how cramped he feels in there right now. But what you don't know is how pleased he is with the modesty of the room. It has no closet. It has no view. It has no bathroom. The organizer uses the bathroom down the hall near the back door.

Tonight you're in South America, in a tiny fishing village, prowling through a back street looking for the woman you're madly in love with. She's run off with another man. You start knocking on every door you come to. People on your side move to the opposite sidewalk.

But it is not long before you are back in your room with the old woman, who, right now is coughing to get your attention. You look into her face.

"The important thing," she says, "is to make sure everything is in place. The windows have to be washed. The dirty clothes washed. The leaves, if you can find them, must be raked. The grass, if it still exists, must be cut. We sit here but there are always things to do."

"Huh?"

"Tomorrow you will probably run off and marry the colored girl down the hall."

"Yesterday, yesterday . . . "

"I went to London, once," you tell her.

"It's not the same. The literature is different there. We have here the closest thing an industrial society can have to the glory of a tribal culture. We still respect our relation to nature. Even in the museum, which I have never seen, you can see it."

You listen to her. She seems to make good sense. She continues: "A lone American girl at the table next to ours. Remember her, twenty-six years ago? Spoke rotten French, speaking to the head waiter who understood English better than she. She ordered a steak, salad, and a cold glass of milk. Yes, she said it like that, 'a cold glass of milk!' And when she signed the Master Charge statement Miss USA I was not astonished. But even that far away—where was it, Paris?—I expected America to have some kind of presence."

You are drifting off into sleep but you can still hear her voice biting at the edges of your mind.

"We grew older. The memory of my mother's hand grows older. The skyline," she says looking out the window, "is black or gold." She is knitting.

You can hear someone passing in the hallway. You remember the sting of the yellow fever shot. But you are not sure. Maybe you only imagined you went to Europe. Perhaps the old woman also only imagined Europe and is inventing it right now.

Nothing is resolved and it is another morning of simple sunlight. You are aching. Your eyes are burning and you know anything can happen. It was always this way.

V
Mobile Axis: A Triptych

Liberties

L IGHT TOUCHED EVERYTHING and thereby shaped the direction of my gaze. I suddenly had a vision.

We enter the bedroom. Standing at the foot of the bed, we have a particular view of its objects: two chairs, five pictures, a mirror, a washtable, a towel on a nail, two doors, perhaps three. We take liberties with what we see.

I have stood in this corner, in this bedroom, many times, overwhelmed by the tricks it plays on me.

In the churchyard I feel nervous. I follow my eyes. They seek the red roof first. Move up the complex lines of the bell tower and down the line of the roof to the far left. Spot the red roof in the far background. It's the tip of a house on a low street that slopes down past the church. My eyes have their own intelligence yet they are pulled back by the footpath and come all the way down to the grass just in front of me. They repeat these motions.

I notice the brooding blue sky and the blue windows of the church. The angle of the light is brilliantly impossible, compositionally correct: the grass around this — the back side — is partly shaded by the presence of the awesome church. Light falls directly onto the church just above the shaded area. This gives my heart an ache it has never felt before.

Is this really the back side of the church? If not, why do I feel such extreme dislocation, even stress? This side of it seems to be engaged in a radical argument with convention. (At the same time, I happen to know that the other side is not as intricate and therefore not as interesting.)

Nothing was consciously planned.

There he is, and I still don't know what to make of him. I have a three-quarter view of the right side of his face. He has the distant look of a man who has pulled himself away from all human contact. He is not happy but feels safe, finally. Perhaps he has just been released from some hospital. It is winter. He wears a heavy overcoat and a wool cap. He is not in his own country and although he might feel homesick—along with his deeper sickness—he is not going to acknowledge it.

He looks suspicious or skeptical or maybe only critical. No, this is a look of scrutiny. Morbid depression and calm scrutiny. I've never seen him smile or even appear to be at peace with himself. Art never makes him happy.

He attempts to recreate himself. He makes the connecting parts work, in a way. In this recreation, the face seems most important to him. Yet he is not about to cry out for mercy or salvation. The face would make you think so. In his recreations of himself—his face mainly—I see what he sees: the limitations of the flesh. I see the uselessness of the material world. I see his point of view—the impasse he's reached. Yet I also see that his aspirations have not completely died.

Has he cut his hand in an accident? The right hand is bandaged. All lines move toward the bandage. The eye swings up away from the hand toward the face, studying it, circles the cap, comes down the right side and takes in the insecure mouth, the collar of the heavy green coat, continues up again, down again, settles on the bandaged hand.

Every time I try not to look, my eyes are drawn back to it. As usual, it's a three-quarter view. The longer I look the more likely I am to change my mind. It might not be a bandage but some sort of mitten.

I've rarely seen him from any other angle. Today his eyes seem particularly close together. They are slightly below eye level, my eye level. This arrangement makes the sharp line of the mountain range behind him very severe in its bluntness.

He has a dazed look. The last thing the eye collects is the steam of his breathing, lifting on the winter air. Despite the furious heat of the background — orange and red — the total effect is one of severe cold. He is obviously extremely cold — shivering, frostbitten.

Everything in and around him is airtight in its relationship to everything else. Spiritual defeat broods in his face, in the seclusion of his mood. He in himself is not a subject matter.

Is his theme suffering?

Are we to find no way to avoid biographical information in these recreations of this man?

Cause is no longer connected to effect.

The Industrial Revolution has yet to happen.

The revolution in interpretation itself? With nothing much to work with, how do we know we're doing our best investigating the nature of human activity or the stars and moon, God and the Devil, the eighteenth century, or the man with the mitten?

We come back to him. He is standing at an oblong window looking out. We're outside looking at him framed by the window. Through the glass we see him all at once rather than in detail. At least at first. It's January or February, as usual. The country doesn't matter but it's not ours yet we live here.

We're looking up at him. Three-quarters to the left. He's stood here at least forty different times. The composition is blunt and simple. A design of squares, rectangles, and one circle, put together in a manner which keeps the eye returning to his miserable eyes. The lines of the blue coat and the arm and the hand — with nothing to do — suspended in the space just below his heart, are hard lines, stretched like a tight canvas. They direct the journey of our eye away from his face and back to it.

Does he possess a sense of himself? What does it mean, in the first place, to perceive one's self and the objects surrounding one's self?

Of course he's not asking such questions. He's into the pleasure principle, being far too smart to bother himself with the abstract side of the brain.

I'm thinking this. When the stimulation of the physical world surrounding him is withheld he becomes disoriented, as has been shown in sensory deprivation experiments I've subjected him to. He waits for his senses to feed him information. Should he eat the cheese? Can he take a shower now?

Nothing has changed. I am his mirror. Through me, he might recreate himself—yet again. The image of himself is no simple model but more primarily my stimulus. The human perception of him as object begs for variety—which is why I prefer to watch, say, a dog walking by beneath the window than to stand here motionless at the fence watching only his motionless, framed figure, in the window. It is a defense against boredom and the otherwise assurance of monotony.

Yet his mission to recreate himself persists. He too selects himself as stimulus and model. But with an important difference: he himself is his most familiar territory.

Knowing that it is not possible to duplicate anything seen, my sense of vision allows me to select from what I see of him in the window. Not all of him is seeable, recordable. To record his emotional substance—the misery in his eyes, for example—I have to arrange and rearrange him, stretch or shrink him, play with the distance between him and myself.

Each of the forty times he's come to this window he has appeared different. You would have thought him a different man each time. Photographs of him taken minute after minute also show a different person. At certain times he seems small for a grown man, at other times, he appears as a very large man, one with thick arms and a bull's neck. His eyes are sometimes slanted. His skin color varies from dark to pink. All the same, he never smiles.

It is several months later. He's at the same window but out here it's warm, so the season is different. He might be too hot in the house with the window closed, but there he is, standing there, as usual. Judging from his expression, he is undergoing some terrible crisis.

Again. This time he's very thin and in a blue suit. He looks like a skeleton. He's holding something — perhaps a palette or a platter. If it's a palette he's an artist, if it's a platter he's a waiter. He's looking out toward me — not *at* me — but beyond, to the left.

High above his head, hanging on one leg of what looks like an easel is a real skeleton. It looks like a mocking replica of his own body. The suspended skeleton seems to be gazing down at the man standing at the window. His gaze is one of astonishment and horror. I can see beyond his shoulder into the dimness of the room. There's a white door back there surrounded by a wall filled with framed paintings. Each face in each picture represents a version of the man at the window.

Women in Love

I T'S A CLEAR NIGHT and the sky is full of stars. There's a barefoot pregnant woman standing in the yard. To her right is a two hundred year-old yardtree in which two nightbirds are communicating —

coo-claws coo-claws coo-claws
pee-cow pee-cow pee-cow

Inside the house, another woman is sitting submerged in warm water in an antique bathtub. She's watching her belly shimmer beneath the water.

Then she climbs to her knees, holding the edges of the tub, and she stands to her full height.

She now appears to be an unmovable mass: made of something other than flesh. There is no way she is ever going to move again.

She is one-sided, about to topple but she will never fall. She will continue to lean like this. Her arms are too short for her body. She could never reach her feet with those arms. Her head is also too small for her body.

Back to the pregnant woman. She has been joined by two other women. One is seated on the ground to her left and the other, also seated, is to her right. The one on the left is breastfeeding an infant. She's closer to me though she seems farther away and therefore smaller than the pregnant woman.

118

The seated woman would have had more foreground had she felt more important than the standing woman. Yet I do not sense that the woman in the background is actually in the background. Rather, what I sense is that in this yard these three women are serene mother-naked beings waiting for godknowswhat.

There is no background, no foreground. All aspects of the yard space are equal. In coming out here under the stars they have chosen also to ignore the rules of retreating-advancing colors. The pregnant woman now reaches down to the grass and takes up a blue shawl and throws it across her shoulder.

The right-side woman is now standing off several feet from the other two. She has her back to them. She seems to be angry, as she glances over her shoulder at them. Across her shoulder hangs a red shawl. She too is barefoot.

The moonlit yard is mostly in shades of blue.

From my point of view the scene might work better rendered in aerial perspective. That would be radical but much like a map showing the house, the yard, the women, trees and bushes. And I might even still be able to hear the birds.

Here are three or four other women in the market place.

In a window above the market is a woman with a mandolin.

The women pick through the green pears, searching for red ones. Meanwhile, the woman in the window leaves, leaving a square of black space.

One of them buys a rabbit and has the butcher chop off the legs and whack the body into four pieces. She watches him with great skill.

Another one is selecting olives from a barrel of brine. She is using a dipper.

This is the climate, as I see it:

Despair, serious illness, dread, anxiety, mortality, jealousy, perversion, dread again, the feeling of loss, the dance of death, loneliness.

At one point in his life an artist I know said that without illness and death he would have been like a ship without helm. A writer I read, once attempted to explain what he was after when he said, " . . . pain and perspiration."

So, the climate contains people.
Here they are:
A sick woman in bed.
A sick man on a road screaming.
A jealous man in the act of discovering his wife making love to her lover.
Men who are judges seated at a long table while a young woman parades before them.
Young lovers embracing in a dimly lighted room.
Broken workmen stumbling home from the mine rattling their lunch buckets.
A grief-stricken man opening the door for four visitors.
The sickbed where the dead body lies fully covered by a blunt white sheet. A young woman in the foreground looks toward a corner of the room. There are large black circles around her eyes. Her long black dress reaches her throat.
Is the screaming man, by any chance, also holding his ears? No. Is a town visible in the background? No.
The screaming man here on the long road does not represent Human Nature but is naturally human. He is running home. Sexless, nearly boneless, bodyless, miserable, he is running home. Everything swirls around him.
(There is the famous photograph of the Vietnamese girl running, naked, on a receding road, away from some disaster. Napalmed and in unbelievable agony, she runs toward the camera. General W. said the child had burned herself on a hibachi.)

So, there was no bridge. Only the road.

But *now* there is a bridge — and it's crowded.
Shocked into readiness, we watch the mob approach. Angst. The sense of desperation in the faces — as they come toward us — is chilling. They are moving in on us.

Our eye level shifts in a most disturbing manner. Nine faces are very, very visible. They are stark, yellow-white, bloodless, pious—and judging from the manner of dress—belong to beings severely distressed and repressed.

The mood of the people rushing us across the bridge is generated most dramatically by an external factor: the sky behind them. It is full of red urgency. They are fast-walking zombies. Grotesque and blunt, carved out of wood, their quest is to turn themselves into water.

When they hit us we are absorbed by their madness.

Again, the sick woman, in her sickbed, in her sick-chamber, is dying. I stand in the far corner watching the comings and goings. This is family grief—etched large. This family has known the sequence of death, from grandparents to infants. Now, the mother. The cause of death? In the old days it was tuberculosis, then it was cancer. Now it is AIDS.

My own mortality hangs on me like the rags on a scarecrow. I feel deeply the effects of the family's grief.

Mourning figures, usually in black, drift in and drift out. They are ghostlike, bloodless, seem barely to hang on. I have seen these same folk gathered and regathered in other groupings, sometimes around gravesites or coffins or other sickbeds, in fives, in tens, in threes. (Dying Mr. Chapman gave away everything he had in fours.)

Usually one female figure stares away from the rest of them, toward a wall, looking as though she can see into eternity. Her sense of loss is incalculable. Her arms are folded across her chest like a lithographic crucifixion. She seems almost ready to sink into the earth while the rest of the grief-stricken visitors move as though they recently broke loose from gravity and are now about to float softly up through the roof and beyond into the clouds.

What amazes me is the stillness, their finalized mood. The massive presence of the floor beneath my feet and the green wall behind the brooding figures suggests a closure which operates as a space sealed off from all signs of life. The light in which we stand or sit or lie is artificial. The room reeks of misery and the smell of decay. I have not adjusted to it nor to the smell of medicine.

Although I have stood here in this corner watching longer than I care to remember, I have yet to see the face of the dying woman. It's almost as though her individuality doesn't matter. She's Death with a capital D. I can see her hair but the covers of the bed are so heavy and pulled so far up around her face that it is impossible, from this angle, to determine anything about her. She might be my grandmother or my mother.

(It was the same a month ago — no, two months ago — when she used to sit up. She sat there in that armchair facing the window with the daylight pouring in on her and at times it made her look healthy. We thought she might recover. I saw only the back of her head in those days. When I entered the room there was always a nurse facing her — washing her face or dressing her — and therefore facing me as I entered to see how she was feeling. It was always the nurse who told me how the sick woman felt. She never seemed the center of her own composition. The nurse was more at center and I had the feeling she'd taken the old woman's suffering and dramatized it as her own.)

It is not I who suffers jealousy this time. It's the husband of my lover. Pity all three of us.

We have stage presence.

My lover is in a purple robe. It is opened down the front and she is mother-naked beneath. I love the swell of her belly though she is not pregnant.

We're in the garden under the latticed grapevines. (No apples, thank you. No scarlet red garments, thank you.)

We're not touching, not yet. Perhaps I am wooing her from this side of the wings. (Speculation has it that our affair is about to be discovered, that her husband, a friend of mine, is about to enter the house unexpectedly, walk through it and out into the garden and discover us together—by that time, embracing under the latticework.)

Call him Stanley.
Call her Dagmar.

Stanley now comes into the yard and Dagmar and I are embracing. Rather than flying into a rage on sight of us, Stanley backs away, stumbles, crosses the yard and stands with his head pressed against the fence. His body seems limp with the emotion that has suddenly hit it from within.

Like figures on a stage, Dagmar and I continue to embrace and to kiss and fondle each other. This is to increase the dramatic tension. The audience loves it and understands all the emotions going on.

Over where Stanley stands are large trees. They and he are in the foreground—at least from the audience's point of view. Therefore everybody thinks the story is primarily Stanley's. He's larger, better focused.
Dagmar and I are ironically insignificant, only villains, in the background.

Although Stanley has no intention of creating a cartoon effect, he nevertheless flirts with it. When he stops crying and lifts his head from the fence and looks toward the audience, his features are rather exaggerated. Rather than wanting to cry with him, the audience is tempted to laugh at his pain. A philosophical trick has been played on Stanley: he is not the serious center of his own universe.

Despite his foreground location, he begins to go out of focus and Dagmar and I come into focus. With the emphasis shifting to us, it is like a painting of a cornfield taking up ninety-percent of the canvas with a ten-percent view of a strip of great historical ruins—squares, monuments, signs of Western civilization far off in the background. In this latter view, there is no doubt about the creator's intentions.

Dagmar and I kiss again. We are locked in a drypoint embrace. Our touch is aquatinted.

Later, we are in her bedroom with the heavy drapes drawn and we stand there against them embracing still. A tiny strip of female light steals through an opening in the closed drapes. I touch the lower part of her belly and she says, "Ethics takes place above the waist, morals below."

I, the larger figure, stoop a bit in order to fully embrace Dagmar. I feel her whole body lifting up into my strength with all her passion. The kiss continues, with her head thrown back, and mine bent over hers. There is a level of selflessness achieved in the moment. It is in stark contrast to the anxiety and despair we both feel when we are apart.

After we make love we go out for a walk, oblivious to Stanley, of course, although we know his anxiety and despair. On Main Street the color vibrations are soft, almost peaceful and the tonic moments of sound are muted and we can hear Abbe Costel matching the tonal effects of do, re, mi, fa, sol, la, ti, do, with colors— with emotions!—such as *do* with skyblue or *mi* with the yellow-gray of Main Street or *sol* with the quiet red of the firetruck screaming up out of Nature.

Our eye level, strangely, is above the horizon line. This is unusual for Dagmar and me because we are not especially tall. Perhaps our passion has disoriented us or things have been moved around out here. It's hard to say. We are literally looking down on the passing cars and the other evening-strollers filled with their own anxiety and despair. The faces of the people we pass are large and red.

There, also strangely, is not the slightest fear that Stanley will suddenly leap from an alley and drive a knife into my neck or into Dagmar's.

Another time. I'm watching dog-tired men leave work, headed home to wives who love them. Their lunch buckets slap against their thighs. They are filthy with coal dust. A powerful compositional line holds them together, keeps them moving miserably in the same direction—out this way, toward me.

I step to the side, fearful they may plunge forward, like slabs of a half-demolished building, and crush me.

They walk in the middle of the paved road. I move to the nearest of the two sidewalks, which is asquirm with monstrously lovely boys and girls with purple and green hair, all eager to be seen.

I lean against a barbershop wall and watch the workers go by. Their appearance suggests hotness and a muddiness that carries exhaustion, a lack of spirit. Packmules of chaos, despair, joyless reflections of each other, they bump along. Monotony is the name of the game. Redfaced, they are vehement and sensuous in an explosion of earth colors—browns, blues, juxtaposed with bloody reds and desperate orange.

The curved lines they follow are not those of Hogarth's curve of beauty—though beauty, certainly, may be found here, as in the call and response of two lovebirds first thing in the morning just outside the midsummer morning window when it is already muggy before six.

They zig-zag, they blunder along, brutal, aggressive, mean-spirited. There's violence in every step. They clash with each other, clash like moral positions at a drunken party.

They remind me of Death on the march. I remember the film of ditches full of victims of the gas chambers and other slaughters, real and filmed elsewhere, and there were curves to those ditches too, as there are curves to the lives of these men, to this street, to their bodies, as they move.

They will work till they die — if they're lucky. In the winter they will shovel snow. They, as charcoal studies, propose a skeptical future for humanity. This is not in any way a glorification or damnation of the working class.

I'm now turning, watching their backsides as they shuffle toward the vanishing point. Still in the framework, I feel the fierce effects. They are impetuous as they sneer back at the punks along the sidewalks and all the while gravity seems to be pulling their dead souls forward, out of the frame, perhaps into a pit (like the one they've just left), an abyss at their toetips.

There's a hazy moon, pyramid-gold in color.

I've climbed the fence of the racetrack. It's just after midnight. Place is totally silent except for a thump wop thump wop thump wop in the distance. It must be a horse. Somebody's out here this time of night riding?

I stay in shadows of the grandstand. The sound comes closer. Then I see the rider on a yellow nag. He's a ghost carrying a spear. He goes around and comes back. He's apparently tirelessly galloping around and around the track under the unfocused moon.

This scene, I know, says more about what remains *after* death than what is hoped to be understood before.

She wears a paint-stained white medical smock, having been unable to find a painter's. At her easel, she is surrounded by five erected card tables on which her brushes, thinner buckets and oils are scattered. The sky light falls across her left cheek and hits the tilted surface of the canvas at an angle she's worked out to reduce glare.

The painter in her studio is working carefully and slowly on a landscape view of an old rotten barn on Route 52 near Walker Valley, New York. Outside the studio window she can hear early morning birds —

> *dippty-sweet dippty-sweet dippty-sweet*
> *swifty swifty swifty swifty*
> *dippty-sweet dippty-sweet*

Here, in the studio, the spirit of the birds get into her work as she paints the sense of the objects — rock, barn, sky distant farmhouse, hillside, tree — and what she achieves here (more than out on location) is a synthesis of the things. Being on the spot might limit her imagination.

(A man is walking across a field throwing seed from his apron pocket in a pattern like music. Behind him is the horizon and the cool presence of firstlight.)

I am reminded of a friend's struggles with *his* sower — a common motif — and his breakthrough with a seated Arab figure, which he considered a failure, but also which, because of its experiments with foreground perspective, opened the way for all decorative painters who came after him because of the way he *tilted* the foreground space.

The Ghetto, The Ocean, The Lynching, and The Funeral

T HIS IS A MAN-MADE world, one so closed off from Nature that the angular patterns seem to reinforce the sense of stone and flesh, hard and soft.

A black minister climbs the steps, possibly toward his own apartment.

Life on the stoop is lively: a girl sitting midway of the steps, a boy also beginning to climb up, holding to the railing. A baby in a carriage, on the sidewalk, sits grimly sucking her thumb. A woman sits on a stone ledge out front of the basement shop where she and her husband stuff pillows with chicken feathers and sell them and have done so from this same location for thirty years. The shop window is packed with big, colorful, fluffy pillows — faded somewhat by sunlight.

To the right of the window is another woman, and to her left there is another one, looking out at the activity of the street. To the far right, two flower pots with flowers grace a window where the shade is half drawn. The women are vibrant black women, as alive as African violets in bloom, as open, as tough, as delicate, and as regenerating.

Aside from the human beings themselves, the only other natural, non-man-made thing in sight, is a tiny patch of sky, with a cloud, reflected in the shop window. Also, it's recently rained. The sidewalk is still wet.

This ghetto scene is built on squares and other hard and sharp right-angles. For all their life, the preacher and the women and the children, on closer inspection, are flat, blunt paper cutouts.

I am alone. I go for a walk along the shore in the moonlight. The moon is a giant squash against a blueblack sky made with layers and layers of silk accomplished with a technique beyond my comprehension.

I've left the house to walk to avoid narrative preoccupations and refuse now to let this romantic moon trap me in a compositional plot much like the one I left at the dinner table. But it's trying hard. You can see what it's working with—the lone boat out there, floating on and at the mercy of the ocean. The message is so heavy it's shameful.

The skimpy boat floats in the dusk or dawn upon the high water of the Atlantic with an equally skimpy flag afloat from its mast. The sailor is lost, directionless. The boat's individuality is distant; perhaps nameless, vague and sketchy, merely passing across my consciousness, sad, dark, and soon to be gone.

I refuse to give in.

The dark water reflects the yellow light and this too is part of the design, this arbitrary story-oriented plot designed to snag me, to pull me back.

To avoid being sucked in, I lie down on the sand and close my eyes, with my hands locked behind my head as a pillow. I now hear more intensely the roaring of the ocean. Possibly it's the roaring of my own blood.

They're hanging a man this morning.
Everybody's going to town to watch it happen. They'll string

him up and hang him from the big old oak tree in the yard of the courthouse. Town "fathers" have determined this to be the most merciful way to end his life. Stories vary as to what he did wrong.

The event will be nonlinear. It is sure to represent selective focus. We will sigh and feel glad it's not us.

Someone moving far, far back from the townsquare, might see all of us, and the hanging as a decorative composition, flat figures in a stark space.

One woman at the edge, in a bonnet, will have that expected high-cheekbone, chalk-white face. In years to come, when she talks about the event, she will always use the third person, saying, "She was there, watching . . . "

Look! There's a funeral procession on the hillside. The foreground figures are more than twice the size of the ones already climbing the path, I presume, to the gravesite.

This is a particular setting: an opened barn.

Visible from some distance, just inside the shaded doorway, an old man is mending a harness. An artist at his craft, he himself is a work of art.

In the romantic tradition, he works with nineteenth century expertise. Manners cannot be ignored.

Even if mending a harness is expressionistic, it is also, at the same time, romantic. Methods and shades and levels of viewing are always present and always take place inside dwellings or inside of experts mending some such thing as a harness.

CLARENCE MAJOR is the author of seven novels and eight books of poetry. His three most recent novels, *My Amputations* (Western States Book Award, 1986), *Such Was the Season* (Literary Guild Selection, 1987), and *Painted Turtle: Woman With Guitar* (*New York Times* notable book of the year, 1988), received wide critical attention. He has lived in various parts of the United States and for extended periods in France and Italy.